LEIBNIZ'S MILL

LEIBNIZ'S MILL

A Challenge to Materialism

CHARLES
LANDESMAN

University of Notre Dame Press
Notre Dame, Indiana

Notre Dame, Indiana 46556
www.undpress.nd.edu

Manufactured in the United States of America

Library of Congress Cataloging-in-Publication Data

Landesman, Charles.
Leibniz's mill : a challenge to materialism / Charles Landesman.
p. cm.
Includes bibliographical references and index.
ISBN-13: 978-0-268-03411-5 (pbk. : alk. paper)
ISBN-10: 0-268-03411-7 (pbk. : alk. paper)
1. Dualism. 2. Materialism. 3. Mind and body. 4. Descartes, René, 1596–1650. 5. Leibniz, Gottfried Wilhelm, Freiherr von, 1646–1716. I. Title.
B812.L36 2011
147'.4—dc22

2010049950

∞ *The paper in this book meets the guidelines for permanence and durability of the Committee on Production Guidelines for Book Longevity of the Council on Library Resources.*

This book is dedicated to my three grandchildren:

Emily, Jude, and Luna.

Where men build on false grounds, the more they build, the greater is the ruine.

—*Thomas Hobbes*

The physicist Leo Szilard once announced to his friend Hans Bethe that he was thinking of keeping a diary: "I don't intend to publish it; I am merely going to record the facts for the information of God." "Don't you think God knows the facts?" Bethe asked. "Yes," said Szilard. "He knows the facts, but He does not know *this version of the facts.*"

—*Freeman Dyson*

The challenge is how to attain, how to maintain, and how to restore a unified concept of man in the face of the scattered data, facts, and findings supplied by a compartmentalized science of man.

—*Victor Frankl*

No objective science can do justice to the subjectivity that achieves science.

—*Edmund Husserl*

Contents

INTRODUCTION

In modern philosophy, Descartes formulated the problem of the relation between mind and body in its clearest form and offered his profound dualistic solution: the mind or self, that which is designated by the first-person singular pronoun 'I', is distinct in nature and substance from the body it interacts with.

Although the major philosophers after Descartes up to Kant did not always agree with his specific solution, for the most part they accepted his fundamental idea that the self and its mental life are not reducible to physical conditions and processes. There were important exceptions, such as Hobbes, Gassendi, and certain of the French *philosophes.* The irreducibility of mind to matter is represented most graphically in Leibniz's metaphor of the mill as he presents it in section 17 of his *Monadology.* Suppose the brain or any physical machine that is alleged to be identical with the thinking and perceiving self is enlarged as if it were a mill, so that we could stroll through it. We would not, Leibniz claims, find thought or perception within it. So the materialist assertion of the identity of mind and brain is mistaken. I do not think this argument has ever been shown to be invalid or incorrect, although there has been no end to attempts to refute it. For that reason, I have entitled this effort to defend dualism *Leibniz's Mill.* Its main claims are that the self is not reducible to the body, that mind is not reducible to matter, that mental processes are not reducible to brain processes, and that the Cartesian view that the self is a mental substance constitutes the best understanding of all the facts about mental life and its connections to the body. What I have attempted to do is to survey some of the central topics in the philosophical consideration of the nature of the self and the mind in order to show that dualism is a defensible position even if human mental life is, in many important respects, dependent upon the body. Dependency is not the same as identity. Nor should one deny that many bodily events are dependent upon states of mind. Many of the major philosophers of the last century—Dewey, Whitehead, Russell, Heidegger, and Wittgenstein, for example—displayed such an antipathy to dualism that Arthur Lovejoy was moved to refer to the "general dyophobia common in our time."[1] At the present time, the general dyophobia takes the form of a preference for physicalism and an unending stream of efforts to reduce the mental to the physical. I see no reason a priori to prefer monism to dualism; the number of first principles that are metaphysically acceptable must be determined by argument and experience, not by the mere preference in favor of one point of view over another.

In chapter 1, I outline the view of the self that I find in Descartes and Leibniz and try to show that it is plausible and not vulnerable to some persisting criticisms. Moreover, I find that the prevalent division of labor between the philosophy of mind that considers the question of dualism and the philosophy of the self that worries about self-identity is unjustified. In chapter 2, I consider the problem of our knowledge of other minds in order to establish not only that the basis of such knowledge is consistent with the position of Descartes, but that it supports dualism. In chapter 3, I take up the topic of the self's own knowledge of itself and examine Descartes' famous *Cogito* in some detail. I find various attempts to deny the reality of a substantial ego to be implausible whether they stem from Hume or Nietzsche, Wittgenstein or Heidegger, or even modern neuroscience. In chapter 4, I explain and defend what Hobbes called "the great deception of sense," in order to show that a consideration of sense perception and the problem of secondary qualities again substantiates the failure of efforts to reduce consciousness to physical processes. Finally, in chapter 5, I tackle the ancient problem of free will and human agency and argue for the conclusion that our experience and conception of human action favor a strong conception of active agency, according to which a free action has no sufficient causal conditions beyond the agent who deliberates and decides. In addition, I attempt to show that there is no valid objection to such a view to be drawn from modern science.

There has been a tendency in philosophy, ever since the Australian materialists in the mid-twentieth century argued that developments in modern science privilege the idea that conscious events are nothing more than processes in the brain, to suppose that physicalistic reduction along with a naturalistic metaphysics is a requirement of science. It has been claimed, correctly, that the tendency of science in the past two centuries has been to exclude supernatural explanations. Laplace saw no need for the hypothesis of God in order to explain the course of nature. I do not take issue with this interpretation of the history of modern science, although I see no need to adopt a dogmatic stance on this question and I do not think, by any means, that the theological question is closed. It would, however, be a mistake to conclude that because theological considerations have failed to win the day in the light of current theories of the evolution of living beings and of the universe at large, science as such rests upon a naturalistic and monistic point of view. In fact, to suppose that scientific inquiry in a general sense presupposes or implies or is grounded upon any particular metaphysical presupposition contradicts what I take to be the fundamental rule of inquiry itself, the principle of rational support. According to this rule, theories are worthy of acceptance by the community of inquirers only to the extent that they are better supported than alternatives by reliable methods of fixing belief.

A reliable method is one that tends toward the truth, that is, it tends to support beliefs that are true or that approximate to the truth; it produces truth more frequently than falsehood. Inquiry in general and in the physical and human sciences in particular relies upon sense experience, introspection, memory, testimony, inductive, abductive, and deductive inference, conceptual analysis, rational insight, common sense, and mathematical representation because these have established themselves as reliable, though fallible, methods that collectively tend toward the truth and eliminate errors. The conclusions and theories obtained by inquiry at any given period using reliable methods constitute a major portion of the metaphysics acceptable at that time. By metaphysics, I mean an inquiry into the nature of reality as a whole or of any portion of reality, as well as a determination of the fundamental categories illustrated by whatever exists. Science is a major source of metaphysics in the modern world. Theories that have become part of the consensus of the scientific community are worthy of being considered for inclusion as part of our overall understanding of reality. The principle of rational support requires that we follow the evidence and the theories that the evidence supports. Whether or not a naturalistic view of reality is supported at a given time by scientific inquiry bolstered by philosophical reflection cannot be determined in any way other than by examining what rational inquiry has concluded up to that time. My argument attempts to show that, as far as the nature of mentality is concerned, neither science nor philosophical reflection supports a naturalistic or physicalistic point of view. Scientific inquiry should not be confused with the various interpretations that philosophers or scientists in their philosophical musings attempt to impose upon the results of inquiry. Interpretations of mentality are just as frequently the products of prejudice or wishful thinking as of rational analysis. In the chapters that follow, I have offered an interpretation that I intend to be consistent with the principle of rational support. I do not claim that the version of dualism that I argue for has no problems or difficulties, although it is, on the whole, more plausible than the physicalistic and naturalistic alternatives. What I do claim is that the current metaphysical materialism has failed to extirpate the dualism that Descartes so brilliantly placed upon the agenda of modern philosophy over three centuries ago.

Chapter One

BODY AND MIND

BACK TO SQUARE ONE

One way in which philosophical inquiry differs from other searches after truth is that philosophy attempts to go back to square one, to fundamental problems and considerations. Other forms of inquiry usually make various assumptions and take for granted the legitimacy of prevailing procedures and points of view. For example, a psychological study of how emotions influence behavior may justly assume that what emotions are and what behavior consists of are well known; philosophy, on the other hand, is interested in examining the nature of the very states of mind and body whose constitution psychology takes for granted. Most inquiries operate within an established, historically conditioned framework, which includes fundamental ideas, procedures, paradigms, and categories of thought that are assumed to be correct and that underlie the basic mental habits controlling the course of inquiry. Going back to square one means that this very framework is made an object of study. Since it is present in the mind in the form of unarticulated habits of thought and action, one task of philosophy is to make it explicit, to bring it to consciousness so that the ways our mind works stand revealed for all to see. Once the framework is understood and becomes an object for thought, it becomes possible to examine it with a critical eye and to raise questions about the truth of its fundamental ideas, the validity of its procedures of inquiry, the plausibility of its paradigms, and the correctness of its categories.

How is it possible to go back to square one? How can one gain access to habits of thought, many of which may not be conscious? How can one distinguish elements of the framework from elements that play a subordinate role? Descartes' metaphysical meditations developed a method of doubt that serves as one plausible way of answering these questions. It is appropriate to consider Descartes' approach here because this method not only aims at raising critical questions about the existing framework but also leads directly to the problem of the relation of the mind and the self to body, the central topic of this study. At the outset of his *Meditations,* Descartes reports that he came to realize that many of the things he believed are or may be untrue. He wondered whether the ways and means that he used to fix his beliefs are reliable. What he was told by people in authority determined some of what he believed, and he acquired other opinions through sense experience and reasoning. Are these foundations of belief trustworthy? Why should one listen to the testimony and opinions of authorities? Do they really have the authority they claim to have? What is there about the senses and powers of reasoning that make them reliable sources of knowledge of the world? Are the things he believes merely opinions that may be true but may also be false, or do they count as knowledge and hence as unshakable truths?

Descartes' way of going back to square one was to suspend the operation of his existing opinions and the underlying framework that contains them, to put them out of action in order to reconstitute his system of beliefs upon a foundation that he is able to prove to be reliable. "If we have a basket or tub full of apples and want to make sure that there are no rotten ones, we should first tip them all out, leaving none at all inside, and then pick up again (or get from elsewhere) only those apples in which no flaw can be detected";[1] in the same way, we should empty our minds of our opinions, many of which are flawed, and replace them only with those of whose truth we are assured. The method of doubt is his way of suspending the framework and its contents. It consists of identifying good reasons for doubting whole classes of belief, such as, for example, those beliefs based upon the senses, for thinking them uncertain and hence not instances of knowledge. In general, the basic reason he offers for doubting anything consists in the fact that we lack or seem to lack a sure and defensible criterion for distinguishing true from false beliefs.[2] The reliability of the prevailing standards that we employ in our inquiries to fix belief may itself be doubted. For example, we have no infallible way of distinguishing dreams from waking life, and we have no way of proving that our thoughts are not being manipulated by an evil demon who acts for the purpose of deceiving us. The supposed criteria of truth that we actually employ are consistent, as far as we know, with the falsehood of the beliefs they fix. The problem is to identify a reliable criterion of truth, one that will yield knowledge and certainty, one that will not be undermined by the corrosive skepticism of the method of doubt.

Having put almost all of his beliefs out of action for the purposes of his philosophical inquiries (although not for the purposes of practical life for which these beliefs are indispensable), and having decided that, since they could not be proved to be true, they should be treated as if they are false, Descartes wondered whether he could go so far as to doubt his own existence. He discovered that the very effort to doubt his own existence proved that he exists because 'I exist' follows conclusively from 'I doubt that I exist'. Doubting is a form of thinking, so the same conclusion, 'I exist', is established whenever he thinks.[3]

Of course, that he exists follows from many other facts about himself. From the fact that he walks or talks, it follows that he exists. But such facts are among those that he has found reason to doubt because of the absence of a criterion for distinguishing dreams from waking life. Thus he must put aside all his opinions founded upon sense perception, and this means that he now doubts everything he once believed about the material world, about other minds, and about God. At this point, the only thing he cannot find good reason to doubt is that he is thinking—if he doubts, he is thinking; if he wonders, then he is thinking; if he imagines, then he is thinking. All of these are forms of thought. It follows from any such fact of his thinking that he exists. So he has come to a place where he is no longer capable of doubt and can assert with confidence: 'I think, therefore I exist'. This is Descartes' famous *Cogito.*[4] He has now found his way back to square one. Since the *Cogito* is itself verified by the fact that it is a self-evident truth, an example of a clear and distinct perception, he has also discovered a criterion of truth that he is convinced cannot fail him.

WHAT AM I?

Having established the existence of that very thing that he refers to by 'I', Descartes goes on to ask, "But what then am I? A thing that thinks. What is that? A thing that doubts, understands, affirms, denies, is willing, is unwilling, and also imagines and has sensory perceptions."[5] Although he supplies us with this list of instances of thinking, Descartes does not tell us what thinking is; whatever it is, it consists of something that these examples have in common. One thing that they have in common is that they are inseparable from himself. That which he designates by 'I', the thinking thing that constitutes himself, engages in these activities of thinking. Activities of thinking reflect his nature, whereas bodies or extended things are separable from himself, at least in thought. Because the essence of the self consists of its capacity for thought, and since thinking is the paradigmatic instance of mental activity, we are entitled to designate the 'I' as a mind, a mental thing. On Descartes' view, the self is not something that has a mind; it *is* a mind.

Shortly after Descartes provides these examples of thinking, he goes on to say: "Is it not one and the same 'I' who is now doubting almost everything, who nonetheless understands some things, who affirms that this one thing is true, denies everything else, desires to know more, is unwilling to be deceived, imagines many things even involuntarily, and is aware of many things which apparently come from the senses?"[6] Descartes implies a twofold identity of the self. In the first place, the very same person is capable of engaging in a variety of mental acts. It is not true that these different acts, whether produced at the same or different times, pertain to different selves. The same 'I' is capable of doing all of these things.

In the second place, these acts of the self are capable of occurring at different times. Therefore, the self that performs them is capable of existing at different times. At one time it doubts, at another it imagines, and, at still another, it wills. It is the same thing that does these different things at different times. The 'I' is not only a mental thing; it is a temporal individual that persists through time. In the technical language of metaphysics, the self is a continuant or a substance.

SENSE PERCEPTION AND THOUGHT

A question arises about sense perception that Descartes undertakes to clear up. He says: "Lastly it is also the same 'I' who has sensory perceptions, or is aware of bodily things as it were through the senses. For example, I am now seeing light, hearing a noise, feeling heat."[7] The attentive reader will note that seeing light implies that there is light, that hearing a noise implies that there is a noise, that feeling heat implies that there is heat. There are two problems implicit in his claim. First, even if sense perception is a mental activity that belongs to the 'I', do light, noise, and heat also belong to the 'I'? Apparently not; these are things perceived, not themselves acts of perception. Descartes, as I have noted, is now doubting the existence of everything that belongs to the external world, the world other than the 'I'. So he is in no position to affirm the existence of light, noise, and heat. He recognizes these problems and recalls that, for all he knows, he is dreaming. And if he really is dreaming, then he is not actually "seeing light, hearing a noise, feeling heat." So he offers an alternative formulation: "Yet I certainly *seem* to see, to hear, and to be warmed. This cannot be false; what is called 'having a sensory perception' is strictly just this, and in this restricted sense of the term it is simply thinking."[8]

Descartes relies here upon a distinction between perceiving something through the senses and seeming to perceive something. If one really perceives something, then the thing perceived exists just as certainly as does the act of perceiving it. But Descartes is interested in isolating what belongs to the 'I' alone. He wants to identify acts of the self in a way that does not commit him to the existence of objects of these acts. So he adopts the designation 'seeming to perceive' that he takes to refer to the act alone without implying the existence of the object.

Having in this way isolated the mental act of perceiving, Descartes asserts that seeming to perceive something "is simply thinking." However, 'seeming to perceive' is equivocal and has at least two distinct usages. Suppose I am taking a stroll with someone in the early evening, and I point to something that I describe as a large dog. My companion replies: "That's no dog; it's a fire hydrant." I respond: "You're right. For a moment, it seemed to me to be a dog." In this context, "seeming to perceive a dog" means thinking or being inclined to think that it is a dog. In another situation, my companion might have asked: "What made you think it was a dog?" to which I could reply: "It looked (seemed) just like a dog." Here I am explaining why I am inclined to think so by referring to my sensory experience, by indicating that my experience was of the sort I might have had if I were really seeing a dog. In one use, 'seeming to perceive' represents an act of thinking, and in the other, a sensory experience.

If I should really be seeing a dog, then I am having a *perceptual experience,* and there is a dog there as well that appears to me through that experience. In addition, I might have certain thoughts such as: "That is a dog" or "What a large dog!" Such *perceptual thoughts* accompany and are stimulated by sense perception; they interpret what one sees. They express what one thinks or is inclined to think about what is perceived. However, they are not themselves cases of sense perception. The proof of this is that the perception can remain constant though accompanied by a variety of perceptual thoughts, some true, some false. 'That is a dog' is false if what I see is a fire hydrant. Interpretations of perceptual experience are thoughts, not experiences. Descartes is correct in identifying perceptual thoughts as instances of thinking, but he is on doubtful ground in ignoring the distinction between perceptual thoughts and experiences. It is the latter that are among the constituents of sense perception. And it is doubtful that they are examples of thinking. Rather they are the ways that material objects, events, and their surroundings appear to the senses; they are the materials of thought, not thoughts themselves. It is possible for one to see something in the absence of perceptual thoughts. Moreover, our perceptual thoughts never designate everything that one sees; the field of vision invariably reaches beyond the particular items selected for attention and interpretation. Perception *presents* us with materials for interpretation. In the light of its interests, the self is stimulated to think about some of the items presented and ignore others. These objects of thought are then *represented* and not merely presented. (Further discussion of sense perception occurs in chapter 4.)

SELF AND BODY

I shall use the terms 'person' and 'self' to designate the type of continuant designated by 'I'. On Descartes' view, the essential nature of a person consists of its being a thinking thing in that broad notion of thinking that he employs. A person's body, on the other hand, is a material thing whose essential nature consists of its being an extended spatial object. Can an extended thing such as the human body also be a thinking thing? It has been known for many centuries that the brain occupies the central causal role in the production of thought, action, and experience. Consider Shakespeare's famous lines spoken by Macbeth as he is preparing to murder Duncan:

> Is this a dagger which I see before me,
> The handle toward my hand? Come let me clutch thee.
> I have thee not, and yet I see thee still.
> Art thou not, fatal vision, sensible
> To feeling as to sight? Or art thou but
> A dagger of the mind, a false creation,
> Proceeding from the heat-oppressed brain?
>
> (Act 2, scene 1)

Macbeth was composed more than thirty years before Descartes' *Meditations.* Even then it was known that hallucinations such as Macbeth's "dagger of the mind" are caused by brain activity. In general, all thinkers of the early modern period who reflected upon the mind/body problem knew that in order for information about the world to reach the self via the sense organs, it had to be processed by the brain, and in order for thoughts to bring about changes in the body, they had to produce changes in the brain.

If a person could reasonably be considered to be identical with an extended thing such as the brain, it must play the central role in constituting that identity. Perhaps we can go so far as to claim that, contrary to Descartes' mind/body dualism, thinking and experience are no more and no less than types of brain event.

Consider Macbeth's hallucination. At first he was inclined to believe that he was seeing a real dagger. But because the dagger failed the touch test, he concluded that what he saw was "a dagger of the mind"; it first seemed to him to be a real dagger, but the appearance failed to match the reality. It was a "false creation," a hallucination. Macbeth ends up describing his experience in a way that cancels the imputation of reality to what he seems to see. Although he realized that his experience was hallucinatory, Macbeth did not doubt that he was undergoing an experience that mimicked the experience that he would have had were he seeing a real dagger. "I see thee still," he says, but then describes his experience as one of a "false creation," thus denying that it was a real dagger that he saw.

On Descartes' view, mental acts are acts of a person or self; they manifest its essential nature as a thinking thing. If we combine this view with the physicalist or materialist claim that mental acts are not only produced by or depend in some way upon the brain, but are actually events going on in the brain, the conclusion suggested is that the self is identical with its brain. Descartes, on the contrary, denied this physicalist view of the self. He was an unrepentant dualist: although persons have bodies, they cannot be identified with them or with any of their physical parts. Some of the attributes we ascribe to bodies are incompatible with those that we predicate of thinking things. But for all that, Descartes understood that there is a close and intimate relation between self and body.

THE INTERMINGLING OF MIND AND BODY

That the connection is close and intimate is evidenced by the bodily sensations or feelings of pain, hunger, and thirst. Here is how Descartes understands it:

> Nature also teaches me, by these sensations of pain, hunger, thirst and so on, that I am not merely present in my body as a sailor is present in a ship [or as a pilot in his ship, in the French version] but that I am very closely joined and, as it were, intermingled with it, so that I and the body form a unit. If this were not so, I who am nothing but a thinking thing, would not feel pain when the body was hurt, but would perceive the damage purely by the intellect, just as a sailor perceives by sight if anything in his ship is broken. Similarly, when the body needs food or drink, I should have an explicit understanding of the fact, instead of having confused sensations of hunger and thirst. For these sensations of hunger, thirst, pain and so on

> are nothing but confused modes of thinking which arise from the union, and, as it were, intermingling of the mind with the body.[9]

The person and its body form a unit in respect to these facts, which show that the self is not merely a detached spectator of what occurs within its body. But because the 'I' is not identical with its body or any of its parts, they also form a "composite."[10] Locke suggests that we should designate the composite of self and body a *human being,* reserving 'person' for the thinking thing. The unity of the composite consists of the intermingling of body and mind as expressed in the fact that certain changes in the body are felt and are not merely believed to have occurred. Individual sensations, whether they have a bodily location or occur in the course of sense perception, will be called *qualia.*[11] Thus a feeling of thirst is a quale, as well as a sound or a sensation of red.

Descartes describes sensory experiences as confused. The reason is that although they represent facts about the body and the external world, they do not do so accurately.[12] When, for example, something looks red, I have reason to believe that there is something in the object that corresponds to the quale; I would be wrong to think, however, that the quality of the object is exactly similar to the quality presented in the sensory manifold. There is something in the object that causes it to look red, but it is not exactly as experience represents it as being. Similarly, when I have a toothache, the painful sensation tells me that something is going on in the tooth that causes it, but it does not inform me of the nature of the cause. Qualia convey information about what is beneficial or harmful to the human being who experiences them, but the information is inexact and needs to be supplemented by reasoning to form a correct understanding of the underlying nature of their causes.

In several places, Descartes speculates about the mechanism that produces the intermingling of body and self. He suggests that a certain part of the brain is where body meets mind and is the locus of causal interaction. "The mind is not immediately affected by all parts of the body, but only by the brain, or perhaps just by one small part of the brain."[13] Soon after completing the *Meditations,* Descartes arranged to have them circulated among a number of well-known philosophers for their comments and objections. Pierre Gassendi was among them; his objections represent the major stumbling block ever since then to mind/body dualism.

GASSENDI'S OBJECTIONS I

Suppose you are looking at a bright red apple; focus on the red color for a moment. According to one view, the color you perceive as well as the perception of it is produced by the activity of light causing changes in the eyes, nerves, and brain. The patch of color exemplifies a quale that has a mental reality only; it is, in the terminology that became entrenched in early modern philosophy, an idea in the mind, an idea that represents those constituents in the apple that direct the light that the eye receives.

Gassendi, a contemporary of Descartes, put forward a powerful objection to this account of sense perception:

> For how, may I ask, do you think that you, an unextended subject, could receive the semblance or idea of a body that is extended? If such a semblance comes from a body then it is undoubtedly corporeal, and has a number of parts or layers, and so is extended. If it is imprinted on you from some other source, since it must still represent an extended body, it must still have parts and hence be extended. For if it lacks parts, how will it manage to represent parts? If it lacks extension, how will it represent an extended thing? If it lacks shape, how will it represent a thing that has a shape? . . . It seems, then, that the idea does not wholly lack extension. Yet if it is extended, how can you, if you are unextended, have become its subject?[14]

Upon inspection, the red quale presents itself as something that it extended; it has length and breadth, at least. But if the mind is an unextended substance, as Descartes has concluded, extended qualia cannot be among its contents; they are not mental things in their own right.

Descartes' reply is implicit in the text of the *Meditations* where he says that "when the mind understands, it in some way turns towards itself and inspects one of the ideas which are within it; but when it imagines, it turns towards the body and looks at something in the body which conforms to an idea understood by the mind or perceived by the senses."[15]

Descartes reiterates that ideas are mental contents, but claims that sensory images such as the red quale are not themselves ideas but are located in the body itself.

In his reply to Gassendi, Descartes develops this thought:

> Here you ask how I think that I, an unextended subject, could receive the semblance or idea of a body that is extended. I answer that the mind does not receive any corporeal semblance; the pure understanding both of corporeal things and incorporeal things occurs without any corporeal semblance. In the case of imagination, however, which can have only corporeal things as its object, we do indeed require a semblance which is a real body: the mind applies itself to this semblance but does not receive it.[16]

In a sense, there is a meeting of minds here between the dualist Descartes and the physicalist Gassendi. Sensory images or qualia are not part of the contents of the immaterial mind; both agree that this would be impossible. Both agree that a visual image is an extended thing that occurs in the brain. For Descartes, the unextended self is capable of becoming aware of the corporeal image in the brain; the idea that the mind forms of this image is not itself a quale; the idea is a pure mental content capable of representing a brain content. In sense perception, the self is capable, according to Descartes, of becoming immediately aware of physical inscriptions located in the brain. Perhaps the physicalist too would agree that the brain is capable of scanning its own contents in the course of sense perception.

However, this agreement leads to an implausible result. It is implausible because there is no reason to suppose that when a person sees a red object, there is actually a red patch located in the brain. No doubt the light received by the eye causes physical and chemical changes in locations in the brain in virtue of which one sees the object and its color. In order to see these things, they must appear to us in a certain manner, and these appearances exemplify qualia. Human sense experience has a qualitative character, which is projected onto the external world of material objects. But, as the exchange between Gassendi and Descartes has made clear, qualia cannot form part of the mental contents of an unextended substance. Nor do they form part of what goes on the brain. What goes on in the brain does indeed produce sense experience with its peculiar qualitative character.

But the description in physical terms of brain states and events does not support the claim that this qualitative character is itself exemplified directly by them. The entities that exemplify the qualitative features of experience are not plausibly identifiable with brain states or processes. Neither Descartes' version of dualism nor Gassendi's physicalism provides a way of understanding the peculiar qualitative character of sense experience. Later (in chapter 4), I shall suggest a way of understanding the qualitative aspects of experience that is consistent with both dualism and physicalism.

GASSENDI'S OBJECTIONS II

In the *Meditations,* Descartes claimed that the mind intermingles with the body, as evidenced by the fact that bodily sensations are among the constituents of experience. In addition, he had suggested that the mind interacts with the body via "one small part of the brain." Because the brain is extended and the mind or self is "utterly indivisible," it follows that "the mind is completely different from the body." Jaegwon Kim reminds us that "many of Descartes' contemporaries immediately pounced on what they perceived to be a fatal flaw in the Cartesian position: How could such disparate substances, one extended in space and the other essentially lacking in spatial properties, causally influence one another, or 'intermingle,' as Descartes said, to form a 'union' that we call a human being?"[17] Gassendi, who was one of these contemporaries, points out that Descartes' conception of the interaction of self and body appears incoherent. "Can one thing exist simultaneously and in its entirety in several places?" he asks.[18] He claims that anything diffused throughout the body must be extended. But if the self interacts with the body at only one small place in the brain, "however small the part in question is, it is still extended, and since you are coextensive with it, you too are therefore extended and have particular parts corresponding to its parts."[19]

There must be some contact between self and brain at the point at which they interact. But, Gassendi asks, "How can there be contact without a body, when, as is transparently clear by the natural light, 'naught apart from body, can touch or be touched'?"[20] For Gassendi, interaction entails physical contact; it is self-evident, he thinks, that two things in contact must touch one another and, therefore, are extended. After all, on Descartes' account, acts of the mind such as willing *cause* motions in the brain, and motion requires touching or at least a physical interaction. More generally, "there can be no intermingling between things unless the parts of each of them can be intermingled. And if you are something separate, how are you compounded with matter so as to make up a unity?"[21] The enormous difference between mind and body makes interaction impossible. "How can contact occur without a body? How can something corporeal take hold of something incorporeal so as to keep it joined to itself?"[22] Critics of Descartes' dualism insist that interaction among substances presupposes continuity in their natures, whereas Descartes' dualism implies such a vast discontinuity as to make interaction unintelligible.

In his reply, Descartes concedes that he had not explained "the union between the soul and the body" in the *Meditations.* He thinks, however, that all of Gassendi's objections to interaction rest upon the false assumption that "if the soul and body are two substances whose nature is different, this prevents them from being able to act on each other."[23] Descartes points to an instance in which it is generally conceded that things that fit into distinct metaphysical categories are able to interact, namely, when a property causes changes in a substance, such as when one body causes changes in another in virtue of the heat or weight of the first or when the weight of a body influences its own motion.

Gassendi's argument against Descartes rests upon the alleged self-evident truth that when one of the items in a causal interaction is physical, one of them must touch the other and that, therefore, the other must be physical as well. Of course, a magnet can produce changes in iron filings without touching them. The moon can produce changes on the earth (e.g., tides) without touching it. Thus the so-called self-evident truth is, in fact, false. One might revise the argument to say that what is self-evident is that when a physical thing causes changes in a substance, it does so by means of physical influences (as with magnetic fields or the force of gravitation), and such physical influences can produce changes only when the affected substance is physical as well. Descartes would simply deny that this is self-evident, and, I think, he would be correct to do so.

Not only is it not self-evident, but, Descartes would claim, it is false, since mind/body interaction is a counterexample. One could go further and say, on Descartes' behalf, that there is a brute, inexplicable element in all causal interaction. When the motion of one billiard ball causes another one to move, that such effects occur as a result of such causes and that such interactions illustrate such and such laws of nature are themselves brute facts of nature. That is just the way the world works. And if such laws could be shown to be instances of more fundamental laws, these laws would then be brute facts of nature. One must draw one's conclusions as one experiences them; one knows directly of effects of body on mind and of mind on body. Descartes would further claim that body is extended and mind unextended. If he were able to establish the truth of mind/body dualism, then he would be entitled to conclude that they interact, even though they are categorially distinct. Perhaps there are continuities among categorially distinct substances, but we can nevertheless be assured of their interaction even when ignorant of the constitution of their natures that make interaction possible.

Of course, Descartes would not claim that we ever arrive at brute facts of nature, because for him, nature's laws are a product of the divine will and God acts always for the best, even though we are seldom able to understand how what actually occurs is for the best. Perhaps we should distinguish between brute facts that are epistemological, namely, those that are inexplicable to us, and brute facts that are metaphysical, namely, those that are inexplicable in themselves. Descartes concedes that there are epistemological brute facts, because God's will is unknown to us. But, he would claim, there are no metaphysical brute facts of nature because if we could understand God's will, all natural interactions would be explicable. An atheist, on the other hand, may admit brute facts of both types. Descartes and the atheist may agree that mind/body interaction is epistemologically brute. Gassendi denies this, claiming that it is unintelligible how such interaction can occur. However, the ground of his denial rests upon a claim to self-evidence that appears to be in error.

One might try to revive Gassendi's objections to Descartes' dualism with the thought that our interactions with one another imply that persons occupy space. When I speak to a person on his cell phone, I may ask, "Where are you now?" and he may answer, "I am standing by the stove in the kitchen." Newton once claimed that every existing thing necessarily occupies space: "Space is an affection of a being just as being. . . . Whatever is neither everywhere or anywhere is not."[24] However, Descartes could reply that persons occupy space not in the way extended things do, by filling portions of space, but indirectly by their relation to the human bodies with which they intermingle. That a person is in the kitchen would then be equivalent to the assertion that the body he intermingles with is in the kitchen. Gassendi, of course, wonders how an unextended thing could intermingle with an extended thing. At this point one should not try to explain what appears to be inexplicable. That mind/body dualism bumps into the inexplicable is not, however, an argument against it, because there are fundamental inexplicable brute facts in all of the alternative views. The materialist has no explanation of how thoughts and sensations could be identical with brain processes; the behaviorist who defines mentality in terms of observable behavior and the eliminativist who would dispense with mentality altogether have no explanation of how it seems to everyone that they are conscious when they are not. It has been said that every philosophy needs a miracle; philosophical interpretations of the mind are no exception.

Colin McGinn thinks that we should not be content with metaphysical brute facts. "What is there about neurons that enables them to determine consciousness . . . ? It can hardly be a brute fact. . . . That is the mind-body problem." Not exactly. Part of the mind/body problem is the question whether mind is reducible to matter, and there is an answer to that. If we should decide, as I think we should, that mind is not reducible to matter, we could then seek an explanation for their interaction. But suppose no explanation is forthcoming. In that case, we might speculate that here is a metaphysical brute fact. But McGinn will not accept this answer: "The problem is how to integrate the conscious mind with the physical brain—how to reveal a unity beneath this apparent diversity. . . . There has to be a natural underlying unity here, for if there were not, we have to postulate miraculous kinds of emergence in the biological world."[25] But why should we postulate anything? As we saw, unless there is a supreme being whose every act is intelligible, then there are very likely to be brute facts throughout the natural world. Every explanation is based upon something that has not yet been explained. Of course, the fact that we have not yet explained something does not prove it to be an inexplicable brute fact; but if we have not yet explained it, then we should admit that it may be a brute fact, and go on from there.

LEIBNIZ'S MILL

On Descartes' view, the self cannot be identified with the body that it owns. It has a body but is not the same as the body it has. Yet the body houses all the physical mechanisms that make thinking and acting possible. The self or mind interacts and intermingles with the body. Can it plausibly be said to be distinct from the body and the nervous system? How can the self be more than a nervous system housed in a body? If it is not a material thing, of what sort of stuff is it composed? Isn't Descartes' mind/body dualism just an example of what Ryle called a ghost in the machine? Who in this modern age believes in ghosts?

In section 17 of *The Monadology*, Leibniz presented a thought experiment whose conclusion, he believed, supported the Cartesian dualism of self and body. The starting point is the fact that a person experiences a diversity of perceptions or thoughts occurring within himself:

> Moreover, we must confess that the *perception,* and what depends on it, is *inexplicable in terms of mechanical reasons,* that is, through shapes and motions. If we imagined that there is a machine whose structure makes it think, sense, and have perceptions, we could conceive it enlarged, keeping the same proportions, so that we could enter it, as one enters into a mill. Assuming that, when we inspect its interior, we will find only parts that push one another, and we will never find anything to explain a perception. And so, we should seek perceptions in the simple substance and not in the composite or in the machine. Furthermore, this is all that one can find in the simple substance—that is, perceptions and their changes. It is also in this alone that all the *internal actions* of simple substances can consist.[26]

Suppose it is claimed that the brain is the thing that does the thinking and that acts of thought are merely episodes occurring within the brain. Then imagine the brain enlarged as if it were a mill, so that we could stroll through it and take a look around. Leibniz claims that in our stroll we would never find any thoughts or perceptions. We would discover many interesting physical events but no mental events. The mechanical principles that brain activity illustrates bear no resemblance to the mental principles that thinking illustrates.

An immediate objection to this thought experiment is that it presupposes an impoverished and out-of-date conception of the physical activity of the brain and of nature generally. Leibniz speaks of mechanical principles, by which he means the pushes and pulls regulating the causal interactions of material objects. But additional physical principles have been discovered since 1714, the year he completed *The Monadology.* If we should stroll through the brain today, equipped with machinery for detecting and identifying physical events, we would find that brain activity consists not of pushes and pulls but of electromagnetic and chemical occurrences within and between neurons. So, one may argue, the thought experiment fails because of its outdated conception of the workings of natural processes.

Will this enlarged modern understanding of what goes on in a person's brain enable us to discover thoughts and perceptions as we stroll through it? Suppose on our stroll we discover a complex discharge D_1 taking place among a bunch of neurons N. D_1, let us suppose, exemplifies a variety of chemical and electrical principles. Are we now in a position to tell what the person is thinking? Is the physical description of D_1 sufficient to determine the nature and content of the person's thoughts?

Consider an analogous case. Suppose you are examining several pages of a text written in a language you do not know. You can discern with your eyes various physical properties of the marks on paper—their shapes and sizes, the color of the ink, and so forth. But none of these features provides a clue to the thoughts expressed. We can "stroll" through these pages as if we were strolling through a mill and have no idea what was being said. We cannot identify any of the thoughts by means of a visual examination of the text. It would certainly help to have a dictionary and grammar in hand. Suppose that none is available and that the language bears no resemblance to any known to you. At first you treat it as if it were a code, and you try various methods for decoding a text that have been established by code breakers. But you fail to connect any parts of the text with words and sentences in English. Your next step would be to consult speakers of the language in which the text was written, if you are lucky enough to be in their neighborhood. Even if none of them knew English, you could study their language games in their native contexts and gradually construct a dictionary of word meanings and a grammar or syntax. In doing this, you assume that their minds operate according to the same principles as yours, so that the method of interpretation you employ is the same as that employed by, say, a child learning his first language.

Let us return to the problem of determining the meaning of D_1 in our subject's brain. We might begin by assuming that, just as the unknown text expressed the thoughts of the person who composed it, so D_1 expresses his thoughts. If we were to press the analogy further, we would suppose that the physical episodes of which D_1 is composed are similar to the tokens of the words and sentences of a human language. Call it a *brain language* and think of the episodes as utterances of *brain words and sentences.* But in order to interpret utterances of the brain language, we would still require a dictionary and a grammar.

How could we go about obtaining them? Merely continuing our stroll through our subject's brain would not get us very far. We could, of course undertake the same investigation that we did in the case of the unknown text, namely, we could study the contexts in which the brain utterances are produced and gradually construct a dictionary and grammar. But this is a long and arduous task, and what we end up with is an understanding of syntax and semantics that is founded upon probable inferences. Quine has pointed out that such exercises in radical translation do not provide sufficient evidence to exclude alternative translations.[27]

The best source of information about the meanings of brain utterances is the person himself in whose brain they occur. If he is a native speaker of English, we can simply ask him to tell us what he is thinking as we keep track of his brain utterances. Perhaps we will come across certain correlations that occur sufficiently often so that we are convinced that they are not accidental. When D_1 occurs, our subject reports that he is thinking that something he sees is an apple. D_2 is correlated with 'That is an orange' and so on. What we discover through this process is the brain-language vehicles of some of our subject's thoughts. The subject knows what he is thinking directly, and that is what allows us to establish their meaning. Therefore, this method is superior to the method we applied to the speakers of the unknown language, since we were unable to understand the reports of their thoughts until we had mastered the syntax and semantics of their language by indirect means. But now we can rely upon our subject's introspection of his own mental world, we can understand it, and we might then think that we were in a position to refute Descartes' dualism in favor of the physicalist hypothesis that thoughts are merely brain processes.

However, even if there should be correlations between brain processes and acts of thought, the latter could be identified with the former no more than the pages of text in the unknown language could plausibly be identified with the thoughts of their composer. The physical text expresses the thought. But the thought is known by reliance upon inferences based on the behavior and the introspective reports of others. The physical text, either in a human language or in brain language, is merely the vehicle of thought and cannot be identified with it. Neither syntax nor semantics can be directly inferred from or reduced to a physical description of the text. The meanings of the physical tokens of a natural language are determined by conventions, by acts of persons that establish meaning; they are not intrinsic to the tokens themselves in virtue of their physical characteristics. And if there is such a thing as brain language, in the sense of systematic correlations between brain processes and thoughts, we have no idea how these connections are established or even if they deserve to be interpreted as illustrations of syntax and semantics.

Let me turn to two recent efforts to refute Leibniz's argument. First, John Searle claims that Leibniz was examining the brain system at the wrong level. He was looking at the actions of the individual neuron or synapse. But thought and perception are global features of the brain involving countless neurons interacting with one another, not features of the individual neuron.[28] In reflecting on Searle's objection, I was reminded of Locke's remark that "unthinking particles of matter, however put together, can have nothing thereby added to them but a new relation of position, which it is impossible should give thought and knowledge to them."[29] We can translate Locke's remark into modern vocabulary as follows: "Unthinking individual neurons, however put together, can have nothing thereby added to them but larger numbers of physical and chemical events, which it is impossible should give thought and knowledge to them." Of course, global features of the brain in which bunches of neurons act in concert will have different causal outcomes than events in the individual neuron. Perhaps thoughts and perceptions correlated to brain events are correlated to global brain events rather than to the actions of small groups of neurons. That is still consistent with Leibniz's point that the thoughts and perceptions are not identical to the global brain events themselves. In our stroll through the brain, we can examine global as well as minute processes; nowhere do we find thought and perception.

Searle attempts to support his criticism by relying upon the analogy of the global properties of the brain with the global properties of other substances, such as water. Just as the liquidity of water is a global property of a bunch of water molecules, so thoughts and perceptions are global properties of the brain. Just as Leibniz could not discover water's liquidity by strolling among its individual molecules, he could not discover mental events by strolling among small groups of neurons. But no one would deny that liquidity is a feature of the water. So one should not deny that thought is a feature of the brain.

The issue, however, turns on what we take liquidity to be. If it consists simply in the way in which large groups of molecules of water interact with one another, there is no reason why Leibniz could not spot it in his stroll through the water. But if we think of liquidity phenomenally as it appears to the senses of an outside observer, then Leibniz would be unable to observe it. For liquidity visually considered is simply the way that the water appears to the observer; and liquidity tactually considered is the way it feels to the observer. Such phenomenal liquidity is a product not of the molecules in themselves but of their interaction with the sense organs of the observer. Without reference to the outside observer, there is no such thing as phenomenal liquidity. It is merely an appearance. Liquidity in the physical sense is not analogous to thought and perception. For global features of the brain—namely, the interactions of large groups of neurons—still lack two of the distinguishing features of mentality—namely, sensory qualities and intentionality.

One suggestion in support of Searle's argument is that, in observing various interactions among the neurons, we are in fact observing thoughts and perceptions, although we fail to recognize them for what they are.[30]

In reply, however, one should wonder about this alleged failure. It is not due to careless observations, since a more intense scrutiny of the neurons will still fail to reveal the marks of mentality. Perhaps if we examined the neurons in the light of some theory about the mind/body connection, we would then be in a position to recognize certain brain events as really being mental events. But it is difficult to know what theory one could offer that does not beg the question. And if such a theory should be one that dismisses mentality as an illusion (such as eliminative materialism), then that theory actually agrees with Leibniz's claim that mentality cannot be observed in the stroll through the brain.

Another response to Leibniz can be formulated in functional terms. What he overlooks in his stroll through the brain are the outside causes and effects of brain processes. For example, Leibniz fails to spot pain because he does not see the tissue damage that causes it, or the efforts to reduce it that the pain causes. Perhaps it is part of our understanding of what pain is that it is caused by damage to the body and that it motivates people to avoid such damage. However, broadening the connections between the brain events correlated with pain and factors external to the brain fails to bring an essential feature of pain into view, namely, how it feels. This is directly accessible only to the person who feels it. Leibniz's stroll through the brain fails to capture the first-person point of view that is essential to bring mentality into the picture.

Functionalism in the broadest sense claims that states of mind are functional states. One way in which a state of mind can be characterized in terms of its function refers to the way it is brought about, as sense perception is brought about by means of the stimulation of the sense organs. Another way refers to what a state of mind causes, as when a desire leads a person to act so as to produce what is desired. There is nothing inherently physicalistic about functionalism. A Cartesian dualist can admit that states of mind have characteristic causes and effects, while insisting that their intrinsic features are accessible only from an introspective standpoint. Physicalistic functionalism, however, claims that a functional characterization in physical terms exhausts the nature of mentality. Physicalistic functionalism is a descendant of behaviorism that attempts to sidestep its defects. Instead of claiming, as does the behaviorist, that mental states are behavioral dispositions, the functionalist asserts that they are occurrent states whose mental nature is explicable in functional terms, while their intrinsic nature is purely physical. Physicalistic functionalism is, however, implausible on its face because it supposes that intentionality and phenomenal experience are completely reducible to causal relations among purely physical events. Consider any true causal statement of the general form 'X causes Y', where X and Y are described in purely physical terms with no mental admixture at all. Let this statement be as complex as you like. I cannot understand how any such statement can be thought to be equivalent to 'Smith is thinking that 3 + 2 = 5' or to 'That apple looks red to Smith'.[31] A thought exhibits intentionality or reference to an object. It has a vector quality as part of its intrinsic nature: the thinker *means* that. When X causes Y, Y comes after X, but that is a far cry from the mental vector of X meaning Y. Leibniz would not notice the mental vector in his stroll through the brain or even in a stroll among the causes and effects of brain events, because none is there to be found.

A physicalist might argue at this point that it is a peculiarity of the human mind that mentality does not come into view from the standpoint of an outside observer, such as Leibniz strolling through the brain, but only comes into view from the first-person introspective perspective. Introspection reveals brain events as they are manifested to the individual whose brain it is. One should not expect that things would appear in the same way from such radically different perspectives. However, this will not do. For what the physicalist calls the appearances of the brain events are themselves mental processes exemplifying intentionality and phenomenal qualities. They are entirely different from brain events because they exemplify quite distinct characteristics. That they are distinct establishes the truth of one version of mind/body dualism, namely, that the distinctive features of the mind are not identical to the physical features of the nervous system. The first-person point of view reveals brain events indirectly through the mental events to which they are correlated.

The failures of these objections to Leibniz's mill might persuade the physicalist to adopt an eliminativist point of view. This means that he will drop any attempt to reduce the mental to the physical and will simply deny the existence of mental states, events, and processes; there is no mental subject matter that needs to be reduced to a physical subject matter. This is a truly heroic effort to avoid dualism, but it is doomed to failure for the simple reason that we frequently find ourselves able to verify the truth of statements that imply the existence of states of mind. Our prevailing methods of verification often give us reason for taking as true various statements about what a person intends, thinks, perceives, imagines, and so on. Eliminativism simples excludes as fictions propositions that we *know* to be true. It is open to the eliminativist to adopt one of a variety of skeptical stances to our prevailing methods of fixing belief, either by denying their capacity to produce genuine truths or by rejecting the prevailing understanding of what it is they are capable of verifying. I shall have some remarks to make about skepticism in the next chapter.

From the inability to find perceptions and thoughts within the physical machine, Leibniz infers that "we should seek perception in the simple substance," the monad. It is simple in the sense that it does not consist of physical parts. It is, however, mentally complex because it consists of a unified steam of inner thoughts and perceptions. When this inner stream exemplifies consciousness, the monad is a person that can refer to itself as 'I', a thinking thing. Thus the argument founded upon Leibniz's mill points in the direction of Descartes' dualism between self and body.

The basic idea of Leibniz's argument is that a person who knows in general terms, and even in regard to the relevant particulars, about the physical processes going on in the human body and nervous system would still know nothing about the intrinsic nature of people's mental lives. For example, suppose a person knew everything there is to know about the physical mechanisms and processes that underlie color perception. He knows what goes on in the sense organs, brain, and nervous system when something looks red to someone. But if he himself had never seen anything red, then he would know nothing of what it is like for something to look red. Or suppose he knew what goes on in the brain when someone is thinking that 3 + 2 = 5. He would not know what that thought was. Even if he knew what it is like for something to look red, and even if he had had that thought himself, he could not correlate it to exactly these physical processes unless he relied upon the introspective reports of the subject or an inference to the thoughts and sensations of another, based upon his own introspective knowledge. In short, even if thoughts and perceptions should be correlated to physical processes, they constitute a distinct subject matter not reducible to their correlates.

I do not believe that there has ever been a successful refutation of the argument illustrated by Leibniz's mill. What it establishes at the very least is that mental events and characteristics constitute a subject matter not identical with physical events and their characteristics. It establishes a form of mind/body dualism, a dualism of events and processes. Does it also establish Leibniz's claim that mental processes occur in a nonphysical substance, the monad? If one denies substance dualism, then one is left with the idea that mental processes are free-floating streams of consciousness that have no home in either the body or the self. And yet we do not consider them free-floating, for we ascribe them to the self without any hesitation. The substantial self is just that point of unification of the totality of thoughts and perceptions that are the constituents of a person's mental life. There is little agreement as to what constitutes the unity of mental life, but that there is such a basis of unity is implied in our ordinary, commonsense ascriptions of thoughts and perceptions to persons.

CONSCIOUSNESS

According to Leibniz, we do not find thoughts and perceptions in the physical machine. What we find are various organs and episodes including, most relevantly, clumps of neurons in the brain interacting by means of chemical and electromagnetic processes. Perhaps these physical events play a causal role in the production of thoughts and perceptions,[32] but they cannot be identified straightway with the thoughts and perceptions themselves. The physiological descriptions of what goes on in the brain entail nothing about the nature and content of any accompanying thoughts. Correlations between mind and brain of course do occur, and these are consistent with the idea that what goes in the brain expresses thought. But expression involves the idea of meaning, and the introduction of such a basic semantic concept is not justified by the mere fact of correlation. We do not find meaning in our stroll through the brain.

One of the things that introspection reveals about the self is that the world, including its own body, appears to it in a qualitative guise. The self is not only aware of the qualia that constitute the content of the ways the world appears; it is also made aware of changes in and features of the world and of its own body by means of its awareness of qualia. I shall use the term *sensory consciousness* for the self's awareness of qualia and *perceptual consciousness* for its awareness of the changes and features of the physical world induced by sensory consciousness. I use *consciousness* as a generic term encompassing all the ways the 'I' becomes aware of anything whatsoever. As I indicated earlier, I do not think that either sensory or perceptual consciousness is a case of thinking. When, for example, I see an apple, I am conscious of certain qualitative features, and, in virtue of the fact that these features constitute the manner in which the apple appears to me, I am conscious of the apple as well. But I may not know what it is that I am conscious of; in a dim light I may take it for a red pepper, and I may have no thoughts about most of the qualities that are presented. These forms of consciousness are not cases of knowledge, although they serve as the basis of the knowledge that is exemplified in perceptual thoughts.

Perceptual thoughts are preceded by perceptual and sensory consciousness and are interpretations of them. But there are thoughts that, in the nature of the case, do not require any of these antecedent forms of consciousness. It is possible to think of the sum of two numbers without any accompanying imagery. One's thoughts about the battle of Yorktown involve no essential reference to qualia. Of course, imagery may accompany our thoughts about abstractions such as numbers and about events far away and long ago, but its occurrence is adventitious and unnecessary in order for the thoughts to have content.

The characteristic that demarcates thinking from sensory and perceptual consciousness and, for that matter, from everything else in the universe, is that it embodies forms of meaning, or what has come to be known as *intentionality.* When I judge or assert that, for example, seven plus five equals twelve, my thought has a subject matter, these numbers, and I am ascribing to them the characteristic that consists of seven and five having that particular sum. Indeed, I am *referring* to the numbers and to the fact of their having that sum. That is what I am thinking about. I shall call this type of meaning or intentionality *representation.* By representing something to ourselves, we become aware of it not via a presentation, as in sensory consciousness, nor as something that is manifested through sensory consciousness, as in perceptual consciousness, but as something represented or meant or referred to; I shall call it *representational consciousness.* This form of consciousness is the essential feature of all thinking, of all states of mind that consist of acts of thought or, as in the emotions, that include acts of thought. A thinking thing in the abstract is a being capable of representational consciousness; human thinking things are capable of sensory and perceptual consciousness as well.

Thinking things are not only conscious; they are also aware of being so. A person may not only be sensing and perceiving something; he may also know that and what he is sensing and perceiving. A person who is thinking may simultaneously be conscious that he is thinking. This is the capacity for *self-consciousness.* Although this is a form of representational consciousness, since it represents one's own states of mind, it is distinguished from representations of mental states generally by incorporating reference to oneself, to the 'I' of the *Cogito.* A person who is conscious of his thinking that seven plus five equals twelve is thinking the thought '*I* am thinking that seven plus five equals twelve'.

In the section of the *Critique of Pure Reason* entitled "The Paralogisms of Pure Reason," Kant claimed that 'I think' accompanies every representation. He seemed to believe that it is a necessary truth that whenever a person thinks that A, whatever A may be, he also thinks 'I think that A'. In our terms, he is claiming that every occurrence of a case of representational consciousness is necessarily also a case of self-consciousness. However, this could not be correct because it leads to an infinite regress that cannot be completed in a finite time. For 'I think that A' is also a representation and thus implies 'I think that I think that A' and so on without end. One might be inclined to modify Kant's view by saying instead that 'I think' necessarily accompanies every first-level representation, but this seems to be arbitrary. There is nothing about the first level that requires self-consciousness that is not also present at all the higher levels. The best solution is to disconnect representational consciousness from self-consciousness. Although one may be conscious of one's own act of thought, it is not necessary that one be conscious of it.

One advantage of this solution is that it allows for the possibility of *unconscious* mental activity. A conscious mental state or act may be unconscious in the sense of there being no further mental act or state representing it. Although the idea of unconscious states of consciousness seems paradoxical, it is, on the contrary, completely coherent. The very same state that is a case of consciousness in respect to its representational function may be unconscious in respect to the fact that nothing represents it.

THE SUBJECTIVE POINT OF VIEW

When Leibniz claims that perception is "*inexplicable in terms of mechanical reasons,*" he has two distinct points in mind. First, forms of consciousness cannot be found within the interactions taking place among the parts of a physical system. Therefore, they cannot be identified with brain processes, although there may be numerous correlations. Second, no physical system is capable of causing conscious activity. Correlation does not entail causation. Even if a particular type of discharge in the brain is correlated with a particular thought, it does not follow that the discharge causes the act of thinking. Indeed, as Leibniz asserts in section 78 of *The Monadology,* "the soul follows its own laws and the body its own; and they agree in virtue of the harmony pre-established between all substances."[33] In opposition to Descartes, Leibniz denies any direct interaction between mind and body. Because "there is no proportion between mind and body," it follows "that the actions of mind change nothing at all in the nature of bodies, nor do bodies change anything in the nature of minds."[34]

Leibniz's thought experiment suggests that a detached, impartial observer studying a living human body will fail to find any states of consciousness. To such an observer, the consciousness of others is accessible only inferentially. Locke supports this idea in the following passage:

> Man, though he have great variety of thoughts, and such, from which others, as well as himself, might receive Profit and Delight; yet they are all within his own Breast, invisible and hidden from others, nor can of themselves be made to appear. The Comfort and Advantage of Society, not being to be had without Communication of Thoughts, it was necessary, that Man should find out some external sensible Signs, whereby those invisible *Ideas,* which his thoughts are made up of, might be made known to others.[35]

Because the episodes of representational consciousness that consist of thoughts and the ideas of which they are composed are "invisible and hidden from others," others can know about them only by inferring their existence and content from facts made visible through speech and behavior. This is the point of view of the *spectator.*

Though the self is concealed from the direct gaze of spectators, each person has a direct access to himself via self-consciousness. The mode of operation of self-consciousness will be called *introspection.* (Locke's term was *reflection.*) In introspection, the self gains non-inferential knowledge of its own activities, of its experiences, and of the 'I' that appears in self-consciousness. This is the *subjective* or *first-person point of view,* in which a person has a direct access to himself *as* himself.

The first-person point of view is not eliminable, as some have claimed. It has been thought that an impartial, omniscient spectator with knowledge of every fact would never come across any unanalyzable fact that makes use of the 'I'. For example, consider the fact expressed by (1) 'I am writing about the mind/body problem'. The claim implies that this fact is the very same fact expressed by (2) 'Charles Landesman is writing about the mind/body problem'. It is claimed that these are the very same facts and that the first-person point of view is, therefore, reducible to the impersonal view of the spectator. Now, I agree that these are the same facts in the sense that their constituents are the same; the person identified by the first-person pronoun is identical to Charles Landesman, and what he is doing is the same in both cases. However, the verbal formulations of these statements have different preconditions. Formulation (1) implies that the person making the statement is the same as the person about whom the statement is made; it also implies that the person who makes the statement believes (assuming that the speaker is honest) that the statement asserts something about *himself,* and that he knows that he exists and believes that he has access to facts about himself. The second statement, however, has no such implications. That there is a first-person point of view that cannot be eliminated from the totality of truths implies that there are certain facts about persons and about their capacity for self-consciousness that would fail to be captured from a completely impersonal standpoint. One may attempt to reformulate these preconditions without entering the first-person point of view, but this would fail because such reformulations would fail to capture the fact of self-consciousness. Formulation (1) does not imply or necessitate (2) because it contains no information about the speaker's identity. And (2) does not imply (1) because the assertion of (2) fails to allude to facts of self-consciousness.

Though the self is concealed from others, it is partially open to itself. Although the mind is to a great extent transparent to itself, there are unconscious mental states, and there is no reason to deny the Freudian insight that the self may have reason to repress some of its past behavior and mental activity and make them inaccessible to representational consciousness. Although such facts about itself were known when they first occurred, the self has the capacity to put them out of mind in such a way as to discourage attempts to revive them in memory, as the phenomenon of self-deception illustrates.

The concealed self exemplifies two important characteristics: on the one hand, its activities are *private,* not accessible to others except through probable inferences; on the other hand, it has a *privileged access* to some of its own activities. Even if it should repress some of its content and conceal it from itself, a good deal of mental activity is quite easy to know via introspective awareness. This is the dualistic picture of Descartes, Leibniz, and Locke. The major disagreement among dualists concerns interaction; Leibniz seems to accept Gassendi's arguments and opts for preestablished harmony, an outcome he relishes because it is one further confirmation of the existence of God, who established harmony in the act of creation.

Let us now turn to the topic of knowledge of the consciousness of others in order to determine whether the dualistic perspective can be sustained against further criticisms.

Chapter Two

OTHER MINDS

MINDS AND MACHINES

Imagine being on the subway during rush hour in New York City. A wide variety of human beings are packed together, some sitting but most standing. A few are reading and talking but most stare ahead impassively. Behind each of these blank faces, we suppose, is a rich stream of experiences: thoughts, feelings, emotions, and sensations that a spectator knows nothing of. The riders have no interest in revealing their inner lives to their fellow passengers, and they are able, for the most part, to conceal their states of consciousness by controlling their facial expressions. Although it is uncomfortable to be packed so close together, you would not know of their inner irritations merely by scrutinizing their impassive visages. But that they are feeling something, of that you have no doubt.

But is your certainty justified? Do you really know that they are conscious, that they see and hear, think and feel? On the dualistic picture outlined in chapter 1, each person is certain of himself. Is he entitled to be certain of others?

Descartes claimed that nonhuman animals, in his time called brutes, are nothing more than physical machines. They have no souls; they are not thinking things; there is nothing that they can refer to as 'I'. Indeed, they lack any conception of themselves; in fact, they lack any conception of anything at all. There is no stream of consciousness going on behind the scenes as there is for the human being.

Descartes supposed that it is possible in theory to construct a purely physical machine capable of simulating the behavior of humans to some extent. In fact, the brutes are such machines. However, there are two ways in which physical machines, no matter how complex, fall short of the human person. "The first is that they could never use words, or put together other signs, as we do in order to declare our thoughts to others."[1] Although machines or animals might emit sounds that correlate with their motions in a way similar to human speech, "it is not conceivable that such a machine should produce different arrangements of words so as to give an appropriately meaningful answer to whatever is said in its presence, as the dullest man can do."[2] The human person can outperform any physical machine because his responses are not automatic or thoughtless but are founded upon a conscious grasp of the meaning of the speech of others.

In the second place,

> even though such machines might do some things as well as we do them, or perhaps even better, they would inevitably fail in others, which would reveal that they were acting not through understanding but only from the disposition of their organs. For whereas reason is a universal instrument which can be used in all kinds of situations, these organs need some particular disposition for each particular action; hence it is for all practical purposes impossible for a machine to have enough different organs to make it act in all the contingencies of life in the way in which our reason makes us act.[3]

One claim on which Descartes founds his argument is that it is impossible to construct machines to simulate any and all human linguistic and behavioral responses. Recently this claim has been challenged by Turing[4] and others on the grounds that for any actual type of human response to questions or requests for information, it is possible in theory to compose a program that will answer the question or provide the information. In principle, machines are capable of acting in ways that are indistinguishable from the ways humans act.

Suppose Turing is correct in thinking that one cannot in principle distinguish between persons and computers on the basis of observable physical output alone. In many cases indeed, computers are able to exceed the capacities of human persons, in chess, for example, and in mathematical computation.

The high school that I attended adopted the practice of punishing students for infractions of the rules by requiring them to attend cube hall on Saturday morning. The punishment consisted in being required to calculate the cubes of three digit numbers, the number of cubes being dependent upon the seriousness of the offense. The teacher in charge would check the answer in his book of cubes; students had to keep working until they had the correct answer. Getting correct answers to half a dozen cube problems takes several hours of arduous and boring mental labor. Today, of course, a handheld calculator enables one to ascertain the cube of a three-digit number in a few seconds.

Perhaps Descartes was mistaken in thinking that machines could only imperfectly mimic human behavior. However, Turing's argument is really beside the point. The heart of Descartes' argument was the explanation he offered for the inferiority of machines, namely, that the behavior of human beings is a product of thinking and reasoning rather than of the purely physical non-intentional principles that cause and control the behavior of machines. The handheld calculator does not think as it calculates. In fact, it does not literally calculate at all as did the students in cube hall. The answers it flashes on the screen are merely physical responses to electrical inputs. For that reason, machines can outwardly simulate but not duplicate the actions of thinking things; they resemble but are not identical to the actions of persons that are expressive of thought, intention, and meaning.

MACHINES AND INTENTIONALITY

These remarks on minds and machines point to the argument of Leibniz's mill, namely, that the principles by which persons act—thinking, consciousness, experience, reasoning, emotion—cannot be reduced to the fundamental forces and processes of physical mechanisms, the brain included. Machines do not represent anything except insofar as thinking things construct them in such a way that their physical processes correspond to the representations that their makers intend.

Consider the handheld calculator that now would be able to relieve the rule-breaking students of the onerous and boring calculations in cube hall by the pressing of a few buttons. The calculator does not wonder what the cube of 357 is. It does all its work by means of electrical processes that in themselves mean nothing. It does not intend the answer that appears on the screen. The shapes that do appear—45499293—are not intended by the calculator to stand for the number 45,499,293. It intends and means nothing. We, who use such devices, have been convinced that they are, for the most part, reliable. This means merely that the shapes that appear have been brought about by physical processes in such a way that they correlate 100 percent with the correct answer, the answer that we would arrive at if we should apply without error the appropriate algorithms to find the answer through conscious calculations.

John Searle claims that the intentionality or representative function of our mental activity is intrinsic, whereas the intentionality of calculators and computers, and of words and sentences, is derived or imposed.[5] While I do not disagree with the point he is making, I do not quite agree with the terms he uses. Since intentionality is a form of consciousness, I do not think that it is properly ascribed to the calculator or to computers or to verbal signs, even if it is classified as derived. The calculator is not conscious at all. It is but a convenience designed, like washing machines and power lawn mowers, to make our lives easier. It is true that we speak of the meaning of words and sentences, but this is just shorthand for referring to what people mean by their verbal utterances. To say, for example, that 'rot' in German means red is equivalent to saying that German speakers customarily use 'rot' to represent the color red. If we stick with the idea that intentionality is just another term for representational consciousness, we will realize that 'derived intentionality' makes no more sense than 'derived representational consciousness'.

Some years ago the *New Yorker* printed a cartoon that pictured a computer printing on a slip of paper "Cogito, ergo sum." The computer 'pretended' to be a thinking thing. The reason why the cartoon is funny lies in the incongruity between what the words on paper mean when uttered by humans and their application by the computer to itself. This incongruity takes the form, first, of the absurdity of the computer's appearing to refer to itself by 'I' as if it were a thinking thing. In addition, the cartoon illustrates the absurdity of a computer's imputing to itself the power of thinking. And finally, there is the absurdity of supposing that something that lacks the power of thought is able to establish its existence by imputing the power of thought to itself. The cartoon illustrates the philosophical power of humor.

The way of sidestepping these absurdities is to recognize that the printed marks "Cogito, ergo sum" really say nothing, even though they appear to say something because of their similarity to the inscriptions of certain Latin words. The computer is incapable of saying anything; it cannot speak; it cannot mean or represent; it cannot assert; it cannot prove. It fails to express any thought; it lacks consciousness entirely. The fact that the cartoon strikes us as funny reveals our understanding of these truths.

OTHER MINDS

I feel sure that the computer on which I write these words is not a thinking thing and that the people with whom I come into daily contact are. Can my sense of certainty be justified? The reason why this question is interesting is derived from the fact of subjectivity: thinking things have an inner life concealed from others; their inner worlds are private; they have a privileged access only to their own streams of consciousness and only an indirect inferential access to the states of mind of others. Speaking now from a first-person point of view, I know that I am introspectively aware of my own mental life or a great deal of it; I can be sure of many of my own thoughts and feelings but can ascertain those of others only by a process of reasoning whose results are far from certain. I may *feel* certain that Harry is angry and Barbara is amused, but my evidence for these beliefs consists in supposed correlations between their outward behavior and episodes of their inner lives that are open only to them. The only basis I have for thinking that there really are such correlations between body and mind is that I find that they hold in my own case. But I also realize that the correlations are far from exact. I am usually able to conceal my emotions from others by suppressing expressions of feeling, or I may simply lack the need or interest to express them. I often assume in my own behavior the blank expression of the riders on the subway. Sometimes I pretend to express emotions that I do not feel, as when I chuckle over a joke whose punch line I do not understand.

It would appear, then, that my suppositions about the minds of others are at best probable and often mere conjectures. My feelings of certainty fail to be justified. Moreover, I am restricted to my own case; the partial correlations that I am able to verify pertain to a single example of thinking things, myself.

> There is much of mankind that a man can only learn from himself. Behind every man's external life, which he leads in company, there is another which he leads alone, and which he carries with him apart. We see but one aspect of our neighbor, as we see but one side of the moon; in either case there is also a dark half, which is unknown to us. We all come to dinner, but each has a room to himself. And if we would study the internal lives of others, it seems essential that we should begin with our own.[6]

But if I must rely upon myself, how can I be sure that I am typical? Wittgenstein pointed out that, on the dualistic point of view, not only are the correlations ascertained from one's own case, but the very meanings of the words used to describe them are fixed by reference to one's own inner stream of thoughts and feelings. "If I say of myself that it is only from my own case that I know what the word 'pain' means—must I not say the same of other people too? And how can I generalize the *one* case so irresponsibly?"[7] Not only can I doubt under the Cartesian picture that a person who is grimacing and pressing his cheek and uttering the words "I have a toothache" really does have a toothache, but I can also doubt that he means the same as I mean when I utter these words. An inductive inference founded upon the examination of only one member of the relevant population is extremely weak and does not merit much confidence. If one's supposed knowledge of other minds is based upon this type of induction, then perhaps one has no such knowledge. And if we would retreat a bit and concede that beliefs about other minds never count as knowledge but only as probable opinion, perhaps we should retreat even further and accept that inductions founded upon so limited a sample fail to be even more probable than not.

It has been suggested that knowledge of other minds has an innate component. Observation of infants and toddlers may persuade one to think that they are "programmed" to respond appropriately in many cases to the behavior of others even before they are able to employ induction or reasoning to determine the mental states that the behavior expresses. A young child cringes in fear at its parent's angry look. It is not plausible to suppose that its fear is a product of thinking to itself, "Whenever I am angry that is how I look; my father looks that way now; so probably he is angry." A nativist may claim that our early primitive knowledge of other minds is an immediate non-inferential response to the behavior of others produced by an innate mental program.

Perhaps some early responses to and beliefs about other minds have an innate origin. Evolutionary theory lends some plausibility to this speculation. But a belief is not the same thing as knowledge. Even if there is an innate mechanism capable of generating a certain class of beliefs, in order for them to count as knowledge or even as justified opinion, they must satisfy certain conditions. In order to gain a perspective on this issue, I shall make a few remarks on the question of the nature of knowledge.

KNOWLEDGE AND BELIEF

What, then, does it mean to know something? Here I shall restrict attention to propositional knowledge in which one knows that some proposition is true. There is general agreement on two conditions for propositional knowledge. First, the one who knows must believe or accept or be committed to the proposition in question.[8] If he rejects or denies it or never considers it, he could not be said to know it to be true. Second, not only must he believe it, but it must also be true. It has often been pointed out that knowledge is a success or achievement. In order to possess knowledge of truth, it is necessary that what one believes to be true actually is true. The claim that one knows a false proposition to be true is a contradiction. Whereas you can believe a false statement to be true, you can't know one that is false to be true.

There has been prolonged controversy about the nature of any additional conditions. It is agreed that the belief that P is true is necessary for knowledge but not sufficient. There are various ways that a person can believe something true and yet fail to possess knowledge. First, he may be merely guessing that P is true, accepting P for no good reason, or accepting P for no reason at all. Second, he may believe P for the wrong reason. For example, he may accept P on the grounds that E is good evidence for P, where E is actually false or irrelevant. Third, he may think that the truth of E confirms or establishes that P is true, when it doesn't.

Whatever the additional conditions turn out to be, they must exclude such cognitive failures. I will not review all the suggestions that have been made, for they are legion. I will consider only one that may have occurred to the reader, namely, that belief in P must be based upon evidence that is true and that really supports P. Clearly this condition excludes the failures listed above. But it has several problems of its own. First, in order to have propositional evidence E that supports P, not only must a person believe E to be true, but he must know it to be true. Something does not count as evidence if it itself is false. There is a difference between having evidence and thinking that one does. So this proposal seems to be circular. Second, some propositions are not based upon evidence because they are self-evident; their truth is grasped—as in, for example, '3 + 4 = 7'—simply by reflecting upon their content. Further, some things may be found out to be true not because of an inference from evidence but by acquaintance with the fact itself, as when a person realizes that he has a toothache because he feels it. Finally, even if we have evidence that P is true, evidence that is known to be true and that in fact supports P, the support may not be strong enough for knowledge but only for probable opinion or justified belief.

One thing that we can learn from these difficulties is that the condition we are after must be extremely abstract. The reason is that there are ever so many different kinds of things that we may know—truths in mathematics and logic, in the physical and mental sciences, in history and sociology, in everyday life, truths that are general or singular, hypothetical or categorical, and so on. A satisfactory conception of knowledge must apply to all cases and not be restricted to just one class of beliefs.

The suggestion that I find plausible is that knowledge consists of true belief that is arrived at or based upon a procedure that usually produces beliefs that are true; it can be counted on to generate truths much more often than falsehoods. Whatever the procedure—whether in mathematics or the inductive sciences, in the use of the senses or memory, in reliance upon expert testimony or eye witnesses or documentary evidence—if it is such as to produce true beliefs generally, then such beliefs count as knowledge.

This *reliabilist account* of propositional knowledge requires clarification and qualification. Let us consider a few objections and criticisms.

RELIABILISM: OBJECTIONS AND REPLIES

One obvious difficulty is that knowledge implies certainty, whereas many of the procedures that we rely upon to lead us to truth often generate a degree of probability less than one. For example, all the swans that I have ever seen are white. Am I entitled to believe that all of them are? We may think that inductions of this sort are reliable, even though we do not accept that we are entitled to feel absolutely sure of the generalizations and predictions they justify. Reasonable beliefs may turn out to be false, and even when they are true, the evidence in their favor may not be strong enough to endow them with the certainty required for knowledge. In fact, the existence of black swans in other parts of the world proves that a reliable procedure is capable of producing falsehoods as well as truths.

It is necessary to distinguish between knowledge and reasonable or rational belief. If all observed swans are white, and if the sample is quite large and varied, then it is reasonable to believe that all of them are. Reasonable beliefs may be false, and, even when true, may be only probable. Even well-supported inductive generalizations are provisional and fallible. Reasonable beliefs are those founded upon reliable procedures, those that can be counted upon to be frequently or generally productive of truth. But in order to have knowledge, not only must the process of belief fixation be reliable, it must be super-reliable, that is, it must invariably produce truth. In that case, the propositions believed are certain.

One apparent difficulty with this account of reliabilism is that it appears to impose such a strong requirement on knowledge that it could turn out that we really do not know most of the things that we think we know. For example, our senses are not super-reliable because they occasionally lead us into error, as thinkers from the dawn of recorded history have reminded us. Therefore, it would seem that we have no perceptual knowledge. One response to this difficulty is that our procedures are capable of being refined in such a way as to reduce or eliminate error entirely. For example, looking at a familiar sort of object in a good light with healthy eyes in the presence of others capable of correcting one's perceptual errors is a super-reliable way of identifying what sort of thing it is. Even if a reliable procedure taken in a general sense is not super-reliable, circumscribed instances of it may be.

In addition, many of the propositions to which we ascribe certainty are not deserving of that status. There are fanatics who claim infallibility for beliefs lacking any rational justification. Claims to knowledge are frequently in error. We often speak of scientific knowledge when it has turned out that theories accepted by one generation of scientists have been rejected or modified by later generations. Perhaps we should not speak of scientific knowledge at all but of theories that it is now reasonable to accept in the light of the available evidence. Such evidence seldom justifies claims to certainty; science produces theories that are reasonable to believe but may be overthrown in the future. Later (chapter 4), I shall argue that certain classes of perceptual beliefs which we are not inclined to doubt in ordinary life are mistaken.

Another objection pertains to the fact that a person may possess a lot of epistemic luck. Imagine someone who makes a perfect score on an examination solely by guessing. It seems that for him guessing is a reliable procedure, and yet we would not think that his answers count as knowledge or as justified belief; they are merely guesses.

What is wrong with guessing is that even if a guess should turn out to be true, it does so by accident. There is no relevant epistemic connection between a guess and the matter of fact the guess represents. There is nothing in the nature of this procedure that makes it reliable: it is not founded upon the right connections to the world. A procedure that is reliable is so because it has the right connections to the relevant body of facts, so that its production of true belief is not a matter of accident. Of course, what connections are right depends upon the nature of the subject matter we are inquiring about.

If a person who usually gets the right answer claims to be just guessing, we will come to believe sooner or later that he is not really guessing even if he thinks he is. Perhaps the way he fixes his belief does have the right connection to the world even though, not realizing this fact, he considers himself lucky. How can that be? one might object. How can one's method be reliable if one does not know it is or even if one thinks it isn't?

The answer is that it is possible for a person to have knowledge or rational belief even if he doubts that he has it or even if he believes that he hasn't. Consider this example. A person is asked: "What is the smallest state in the United States?" At first, he hesitates and then says: "I am not sure. I guess Rhode Island." Of course, he is correct. And it turns out that this is something that he learned years ago in school but forgot about the fact that he had learned it. He thought he was just guessing when in reality he knew the right answer. Consider the philosophical skeptic who denies that he knows anything even though there are, in reality, lots of things he knows.

But this answer leads to another objection. If a person does not realize that the way he fixes his belief is reliable or is not able to explain why it is reliable, how can he be in a position to justify his belief to others?

The answer is that sometimes one cannot justify it to others. Sometimes a person is in a position to know something in virtue of the kind of thing it is—such as knowledge of one's own thoughts—even though he is not capable of proving that he has such knowledge or explaining why his procedure is reliable or super-reliable. He may not even know the nature of the process by which he fixes his belief. And even when one knows what the process is, there may be many things about it that are unknown, as in the case of perceptual consciousness. There is simply a difference between being in possession of knowledge and understanding all the conditions that enable one to possess it. Such conditions, varying from case to case and often unknown, are too specific to be incorporated into a conception of knowledge suitable for all cases.

As far as being able to justify one's opinion to others, perhaps one cannot always do so. At some point the process of justification comes to an end.[9] Being able to justify one's belief to others is not among the general conditions of knowledge. Of course, there are some inquiries, such as science or philosophy or mathematics, in which a person is not entitled to participate unless he is able to provide a justification—even a fragmentary one—to others. Membership in the community of inquirers usually requires an ability to articulate one's reasons for or against the views being considered. Even here there are exceptions. Consider the story about the well-known mathematician who wrote a formula on the blackboard, saying that it was intuitively obvious. One of his students questioned whether it was indeed self-evident. After reflecting for a while, the teacher answered: "Yes, it is."

A SKEPTICAL INTERLUDE

A fundamental objection to reliabilism is founded upon skeptical challenges. Beliefs are justified to the extent that they are based upon reliable processes or procedures or methods of fixing belief. A super-reliable procedure produces knowledge. But how can we know or be sure that any of our prevailing methods of fixing beliefs are reliable or super-reliable?

For example, perceptual beliefs are justified because the sensory processes that ground perception produce beliefs that are usually true. But how does one know that? Well, we remember that perception does not usually lead us astray. But now, says the skeptic, the claim that perception is reliable is founded upon memory. How can one establish that memory is trustworthy? Any reason for trusting one method of fixing belief will be founded upon some other method of fixing belief that is deemed to be reliable. Every response to a skeptical challenge will be vulnerable to the same challenge. Every reply to skepticism will rest upon an assumption that the skeptic claims is unjustified. But knowledge or justified belief cannot rest upon an assumption that is not justified. Radical skepticism concludes, therefore, that we do not possess the knowledge or reasonable beliefs we take ourselves to possess.

I pointed out in the previous section that it is not part of the general conditions of knowledge that one must be able to justify a claim to knowledge to one who challenges it. That one is not able to prove or establish without assumption that one has knowledge does not prove that one does not have it. One's belief can both be true and be based upon a reliable or super-reliable foundation even if one cannot prove it. Skepticism imposes too strong a condition upon knowledge, namely, that one can always prove that one has it.

In fact, skepticism asks for the impossible. Every time that one tries to answer a skeptical challenge to some method of fixing belief, one must use a method of fixing belief. The skeptic can always challenge any method one employs in the regress of conditions. The skeptic asks for a proof that any method is reliable without using a method whose reliability can be challenged. Since any method can be challenged to prove its credentials, in order to satisfy the skeptic, one must complete a self-contradictory task.

In addition, skepticism is caught in a web of logical incoherence. The skeptic offers an argument with a conclusion that he endorses. He claims that the argument proves the conclusion. But the conclusion is that knowledge is impossible. So he *knows* that he has no knowledge.

Radical skepticism is caught in a dilemma. It offers its doubts either without argument or with argument. If it offers them without argument, then it fails to provide any reason for thinking them to be justified. Skepticism is just a dogmatic assertion. If it presents arguments, then it attempts to prove that its conclusions are true or at least justified. But then it uses a procedure vulnerable to its own challenge, and it contradicts its claim that knowledge is impossible.

Of course, skepticism in its dogmatic form may be true though unjustified. It is logically possible that there are no reliable or super-reliable procedures at all. There is no contradiction in that supposition. But the fact that skepticism may be formulated in a consistent form does not establish that we do not have a good deal of knowledge based upon reliable methods. We have plenty of reason for thinking that the procedures we unhesitatingly use in science and in daily life to fix our beliefs are reliable. We are able to appeal to reliable methods to support claims that our procedures are reliable. Of course, the skeptic will assert that these efforts to establish reliability either generate an unending regress or will end in a circle; in either case, we fail to prove reliability. But if any of the methods we use to show that other methods are reliable are themselves reliable, then indeed we possess beliefs that are justified. For example, if I appeal to memory to show that perception is reliable, and if memory is reliable, then I am justified in thinking that perception is reliable. The fact that I have not and perhaps cannot prove memory to be reliable without circularity does not show that it is not reliable or that perception is not reliable.

Radical skepticism is correct in one respect. We cannot prove that we have knowledge or justified belief under the conditions the skeptic lays down. But these conditions ask for the impossible, and the failure to satisfy them does not refute our claim to be in possession of knowledge.

Those who are impressed by skeptical arguments but are unwilling to draw radical skeptical conclusions may think of themselves as rejecting, not justified belief, but absolute certainty. They may be inclined to adopt a probabilistic approach to the problem of knowledge. Even if we cannot attain certainty, many of our beliefs in everyday life and science can be justified by reference to evidence showing them to be more likely than not. Peirce entitled his version of probabilistic epistemology *fallibilism:* "For fallibilism is the doctrine that our knowledge is never absolute but always swims, as it were, in a continuum of uncertainty and indeterminacy."[10]

Suppose I have flipped a coin many times and, because it came up heads one half the time and tails the other half, I am convinced that the coin is fair and that the probability of either heads or tails coming up in the future is exactly one half. Is that probability claim something that I know to be true? Is certainty about probability possible? A consistent fallibilist in Peirce's tradition would have to say that there is no certainty even about probabilities. In that case, there is no such thing as knowledge, not even about fallibilism. How, then, does that view differ from skepticism?

It is difficult to sustain a stable position between skepticism and dogmatism. For example, Quine pointed out that when we encounter some fact that contradicts something we already believe, the logical principle of non-contradiction requires us to reconsider the truth-values that we have imputed to our beliefs. Some things that we believed to be true will now be rejected as false, and, perhaps, some things we had rejected as false we will come to accept as true. According to Quine, "the total field is so underdetermined by its boundary conditions, experience, that there is much latitude of choice as to what statements to reevalute in the light of any single contrary experience."[11] A recalcitrant experience provides us with the opportunity to reconsider the epistemic value of our beliefs. This opportunity consists of making a choice. We can choose to accept this and reject that, or we can choose to reject this and accept that. Empirical evidence does not determine what choice we are to make (another result of skeptical argumentation) because it does not logically imply which elements of the theory in question are at fault. Experience shows that something is amiss, but it is up to us to rearrange things as best we can.

In the light of the fact that it is up to us, Quine reasons:

> Any statement can be held true come what may, if we make drastic enough adjustments elsewhere in the system. Even a statement very close to the [experiential] periphery can be held true in the face of recalcitrant experience by pleading hallucination or by amending certain statements of the kind called logical laws. Conversely, by the same token, no statement is immune from revision.[12]

According to this version of fallibilism, logic itself can be amended in order to eliminate the contradiction between theory and experience as long as we conform to "our natural tendency to disturb the total system as little as possible."[13] Such conformity, however, is a requirement of convenience, not a condition of objective truth.

One does not find in Quine's account of belief revision any place for certainty or even knowledge. If I know that a proposition P is true, then P is true and I am not entitled to reevaluate it as false. If I should now take it as false, I am not merely exercising free choice; I have made a mistake. Quine's picture of our epistemic condition makes it difficult to understand how mistakes can occur in the process of belief revision. The suggestion that anything goes as long as we conform to our natural tendencies seems indistinguishable from Hume's skepticism. Unlike the ancient Pyrrhonists, Quine does not insist that we refrain from forming opinions. But it is difficult to understand how any system of belief is epistemically superior to any other if we have such wide latitude in choosing what to believe. Even the logical condition that an acceptable system must be consistent with experience is not much of a requirement, considering the fact that, since there are no self-evident logical principles, nothing but convenience stands in the way of revising them, and any experience can be declared an illusion.

The way to escape both skepticism and dogmatism is to adopt the position of reliabilism. Reliabilism allows for knowledge and certainty as well as probability. It thinks of belief revision not just as a matter of choice conforming to constraints of expediency, but as an effort to find out the ways the world really works in the light of tested procedures applied throughout history by the community of inquirers. It is not dogmatic because it fixes belief by reference to procedures that we have reason to think tend toward truth.

An infallibilist with respect to some opinion or other claims that he could not be mistaken. A reliabilist, on the other hand, need claim only that he is not mistaken. Unlike the infallibilist, he denies that he is immune from the possibility of error. But neither does he doubt that he possesses knowledge and justified belief when everything points to his possessing them. This is a more acceptable version of fallibilism than one that privileges uncertainty as the main fact of our epistemic life.

THE BEETLE IN THE BOX

We are now in a position to reply to Wittgenstein's question, "How can I generalize the *one* case so irresponsibly?" The fact of the matter is that any inductive procedure begins with one case. I see a white swan for the first time; I am inclined to believe that swans in general are white. This is not a case of epistemic irresponsibility; it is merely a suggestion that has entered my mind. Induction is a procedure whereby experience suggests general or statistical truths and then confirms them, or refutes them, or refines our conception of the correct ratio. It is reliable in the sense that continued applications of induction tend to approach the actual ratio exemplified in the total population. By induction I mean the mental tendency (which natural selection has likely made part of the innate program of our minds) to extrapolate the ratio of an observed sample onto the whole population, observed or not. Its reliability increases as the sample gets larger and more diverse and if it is selected at random.

One problem with assessing the reliability of induction is a consequence of the thought broached by Whitehead that the laws of nature might not be permanent.[14] It is possible that the habits of nature vary from one cosmic epoch to another. Perhaps in a billion years, the structures of matter will evolve so that the force of gravity will apply not inversely as the square of the distance but as the cube of the distance. This idea suggests that we should be modest in our claims about the temporal extent of our inductive extrapolations. A dose of fallibilism is warranted in the assessment of our epistemic condition. By all means, restrict our extrapolations to this cosmic epoch; that is long enough for all practical purposes.

A further problem arises in the special case of applying induction to fix beliefs about other minds. In the case of the swans, the correlations that are extrapolated between the type of bird and its color are observed. However, the thoughts and feelings of another are not observed. One member of the correlation is invisible. I see a person's facial expression and become inclined to think he is in a rage. I do not observe his rage, however. What I extrapolate is a correlation between his manner of behavior and an inner mental episode in which only one of the correlated events is observable. The other is an inferred supposition.

It is customary to label this type of reasoning as inference to the best explanation, or abduction. Nothing explains this person's behavior better than the hypothesis that he is in a rage. Inductive extrapolation then generalizes the connection established by abductive inference.

But why should we suppose that it is rage that explains his behavior best of all? Perhaps electrical events in his nervous system are responsible for his behavior without the intervention of any mental state. Moreover, if the mental states of others are invisible, then a spectator is able to grasp their nature only from an introspective awareness of his own state of mind. One is confined to one's own case not only for the initial grounds of the inductive extrapolation of the correlations between mind and behavior but also for a grasp of the nature of the mental correlate.

Wittgenstein argues that this whole picture is mistaken:

> Now someone tells me that *he* knows what pain is only from his own case!—Suppose everyone had a box with something in it: we call it a "beetle". No one can look into anyone else's box, and everyone says he knows what a beetle is only by looking at *his* beetle.—Here it would be quite possible for everyone to have something different in his box. One might even imagine such a thing constantly changing.—But suppose the word "beetle" had a use in these people's language?—If so it would not be used as the name of a thing. The thing in the box has no place in the language game at all; not even as a *something:* For the box might even be empty.[15]

Wittgenstein's argument is an attempted *reductio ad absurdum* of the claim of classical mind/body dualism that one grasps the nature of a mental state such as pain only from one's own case. For if that were true, one would have no right to think that others have the same thing that one has, or that others have anything at all.

It is true that the presumption that the "beetles" others have resemble one's own or that others have "beetles" at all is not highly confirmed by the initial extrapolation from one's own case. One is not entitled epistemically to be certain about what others have in their box. One can easily introduce doubts here. But, says Wittgenstein, from a practical point of view, doubt may be inappropriate. "Just try—in a real case—to doubt someone else's fear or pain."[16]

Wittgenstein's point seems to be that the absence of doubt in our everyday language games about pain or fear or other states of mind is incompatible with the dualistic model. That model makes it impossible to have any knowledge about other minds: "The conclusion was only that a nothing would serve just as well as a something about which nothing could be said."[17]

Is Wittgenstein denying that there is an inner life accompanying outer behavior? His interlocutor asks: "'But you will surely admit that there is a difference between pain-behaviour accompanied by pain and pain-behaviour without any pain?'" He replies: "Admit it? What greater difference could there be?"[18] Wittgenstein does not, apparently, deny that there is an inner mental life that accompanies outer behavior. He appears to reject behaviorism. He does not want to deny obvious facts of our mental life.

> What gives the impression that we want to deny anything? . . . The impression that we wanted to deny something arises from our setting our faces against the picture of the 'inner process'. What we deny is that the picture of the inner process gives us the correct idea of the use of the word "to remember". We say that this picture with its ramifications stands in the way of our seeing the use of the word as it is.[19]

How is it possible to reject the dualistic model without embracing behaviorism or something similar? Wittgenstein says of pain, "It is not a *something*, but not a nothing either!"[20] How can he overcome this seeming paradox?

He answers: "The paradox disappears only if we make a radical break with the idea that language always functions in one way, always serves the same purpose: to convey thoughts—which may be about houses, pains, good and evil, or anything else you please."[21] What causes the difficulty is the view that words are invariably referential. "If we construe the grammar of the expression of sensation on the model of 'object and designation' the object drops out of consideration as irrelevant."[22] Both dualism and behaviorism construe the grammar of the expression of sensation in this way. So does the mind/brain identity theory. By assuming that 'pain' designates some entity, each of these theories offers an interpretation of its nature. But if we adopt another approach to language, one that accepts that there is a multiplicity of linguistic functions, then we need not be forced to suppose that 'pain' is the name of something. If it is not a name, then we do not have to posit anything for it to name.

Wittgenstein is committed to our everyday language games. He does not try to undermine them by philosophical reason, nor does he propose to reduce them to something other than they appear to be. But in such language games, we do frequently speak of states of mind as if something were actually going on. Further, we understand that others are often capable of concealing what is going on. When we begin our philosophical reflections about the nature of mental things, we quickly raise questions about their real nature, questions that are difficult to answer and, given the prolonged discussion about them in the philosophical tradition, perhaps unanswerable.

Wittgenstein believes that when philosophers get stuck in this way, they have made a big mistake. Here is how he understands it:

> How does the philosophical problem about mental processes and states and about behaviourism arise?—The first step is the one that altogether escapes notice. We talk of processes and states and leave their nature undecided. Sometimes perhaps we shall know more about them—we think. But that is just what commits us to a particular way of looking at the matter. For we have a definite concept of what it means to learn to know a process better. (The decisive movement in the conjuring trick has been made, and it was the very thing that we thought quite innocent.)—And now the analogy which was to make us understand our thoughts falls to pieces. So we have

> to deny the yet uncomprehended process in the yet unexplored medium. And now it looks as if we had denied mental processes. And naturally we don't want to deny them.[23]

What exactly is the conjuring trick that, according to Wittgenstein, produces the mistaken model of the mind? What is it that produces "a particular way of looking at the matter"?

It consists, I think, of three philosophical steps. First, we suppose that behavior is an expression of mental processes and states. Second, our supposition that there are such things to be expressed leaves open how their nature is to be understood. Third, we suppose further that we will learn more about them upon subsequent investigation. This seems reasonable because we understand what is involved in learning more about a process whose existence is not in doubt. This is the conjuring trick.

But what exactly is wrong with these suppositions? Wittgenstein speaks of "the analogy, which was to make us understand our thoughts." I interpret him here to mean that we suppose that there is a resemblance between the mental processes that underlie behavior and other processes whose nature is left to further investigation. The philosophical problem about the mind and about behaviorism arises as a consequence of thinking that there is a further philosophical problem involved, namely, the problem of understanding the nature of these mental processes. Are they processes in the brain, or do they occur in a different medium entirely? The problem of behaviorism arises because behaviorism insists they are to be identified with behavior rather than something inner. But, as we saw, Wittgenstein does not reject our ordinary language games, even though he has set himself "against the picture of the 'inner process.'"

The conjuring trick consists of what Wittgenstein takes to be the false presupposition that underlies the raising of these questions, namely, that the terms we use to talk about the mind, such as 'pain', 'fear', and 'memory', are names that designate objects. Since that is not how they function, we should abandon the philosophical quest to discover the real nature of the "uncomprehended process in the yet unexplored medium." The belief that there is something to discover rests upon a mistaken picture of the workings of our language games.

KNOWLEDGE OF OTHER MINDS

Wittgenstein's *Philosophical Investigations* begins with a lengthy passage in Latin from Augustine's *Confessions.* He interprets it as follows:

> These words, it seems to me, give us a particular picture of the essence of human language. It is this: the individual words in language name objects—sentences are combinations of such names.—In this picture of language we find the roots of the following idea: Every word has a meaning. This meaning is correlated with the word. It is the object for which the word stands.[24]

We saw that Wittgenstein sets himself against this picture. Instead, we should "make a radical break with the idea that language always functions in one way." With regard to the mind/body problem, Wittgenstein proposes that we should abandon trying to interpret talk of sensations "on the model of 'object and designation.'"

That the general picture of language Wittgenstein ascribes to Augustine is mistaken is now generally accepted. Wittgenstein, J. L. Austin, and many others have convinced the philosophical community that language has a multiplicity of functions and that referring to objects and making assertions are not the only things we do with words. However, that there is a multiplicity of functions is not sufficient to justify abandoning the idea that 'pain' and 'sensation' are names of inner states. Our ordinary language games do not compel us to surrender the picture of the inner process. We certainly speak of pains and sensations generally as episodes that occur in various parts of the body. And we certainly think that there is more to know about them. A good deal of psychology studies sensations and their relations to processes in the nervous system and to external and somatic stimuli. Philosophical problems gradually emerge when we wonder whether sensations are to be identified with the neural events that we discover to be correlated with them. Difficulties with the mind/brain identity theory lead us to take seriously the dualism of Descartes and Leibniz. But the alleged implausibility of dualism is a reason to explore the behaviorist alternative. Philosophical problems about the mind are not products of an erroneous conception of how language works, as Wittgenstein thinks, but arise naturally as we reflect upon our ordinary language games. The transition to the model of the inner process is natural and is forced upon us as other pictures fail to survive criticism. Rather than being just a conjuring trick, the three steps that Wittgenstein considers to rest upon a mistaken presupposition about language are natural extensions of ordinary talk about the mind and do not violate any rules of linguistic usage. Our ordinary talk leads us to favor the picture of the inner process. Instead of lamenting the direction that Descartes gave to the mind/body problem, we should congratulate him for placing the problem of consciousness on the agenda of modern science and philosophy.

Another argument suggested by some of Wittgenstein's remarks requires consideration. It is that the epistemic condition of our knowledge of other minds due to the picture of the inner process clashes with our practical life. We do not characteristically doubt, in fact we frequently feel quite confident about, what is going on in the minds of others. We come to the aid of a person in pain. We do not stop to wonder whether he is just a robot in human guise. Yet, it would seem, we are not entitled to this level of confidence. Our prevailing inductive and abductive methods justify only probabilistic conclusions. From an epistemic point of view, our beliefs about other minds are far from certain. Our evidence does not in itself contradict the idea that others have no beetles in their boxes. Perhaps others are just robots or machines regulated by purely physical principles, as Descartes understood nonhuman animals to be.

However, such a clash need not compel us to adopt Wittgenstein's "radical break" with our ordinary understanding of mentalistic discourse. It is not unusual for practical considerations to justify actions that we might be reluctant to adopt on the basis of the evidence alone. For example, we might wonder whether or not a whole population should be vaccinated to protect them against a dangerous illness, even though the evidence does not prove that the danger is imminent. Should I go to the emergency room because of chest pains, even though they may only be due to indigestion? Practical exigencies and considerations of risk may force our hand when evidence alone yields only modest probabilities.

Another difficulty with the use of inductive and abductive procedures to fix belief about other minds is that their conclusions cannot be directly confirmed. Is John acting that way because he is enraged? I think that is what is going on, but since his rage is invisible and directly accessible only to John's own introspection, I cannot prove that I am on the right track. And even if I am, I am in no position to establish beyond a reasonable doubt that I am. Only John really knows what passes through his mind. Others are only entitled to a belief founded upon a type of evidence whose reliability cannot be checked.

It is, of course, not unusual in science for the conclusions of abductive inferences to be accepted in the absence of direct verification. The world as understood by the physical sciences is populated by unobservable entities whose existence is posited as the best explanation of a variety of observable and experimental phenomena. The widely accepted hypothesis of the big bang origination of the universe is one example. Quantum indeterminacy is another. Such conditions are known by their observable effects and only by their observable effects. Even when direct verification is unavailable or even technically or nomologically impossible, indirect verification is capable of convincing us of the truth of such hypotheses. Predicted events are observed to occur; alternative explanations are falsified; support is increased via systematic coherence with our preexisting conceptions. In just that way, we confirm that John's behavior is an expression of his rage. An enraged person acts differently from one who is in an agreeable mood, and each such act further confirms the hypothesis of rage. Strange as it may seem, John's rage and the big bang are in the same epistemic boat, although the former may set us a practical problem that does not arise with the latter.

Throughout this discussion, I have been assuming a *realistic understanding* of the outcomes of inductive and abductive inference. The claims they justify entail various ontological commitments, and this means that they justify belief in the reality of the objects and events whose existence is entailed. There are, however, many philosophers who have adopted versions of *anti-realism* because of the absence of direct verification of the existence of unobservables. Quine once spoke of unobservables as convenient myths whose epistemic rationale is to simplify our theories rather than to reflect the essence of a transcendent reality.[25] Pragmatists and instrumentalists interpret scientific theories as devices for predicting the future. Phenomenalists accept the reality only of what is directly observable and consider theories to be merely shorthand descriptions of experiential events.

The general difficulty with all forms of anti-realism is that they imply radical skepticism. Our knowledge of the existence and properties of bodies is founded upon sense experience. Our beliefs about bodies refer mostly to facts about them that hold even when no one is observing them. Our commonsense beliefs as well as our scientific theories about nature and the human world are founded upon inductive and abductive inference and transcend direct verification. Our beliefs about the past that are fixed by recollection and testimony are similarly justified by probabilistic inference, as are beliefs about the future and other minds. Thus, the main argument for anti-realism, according to which only direct observation provides a rational basis for ontological commitment, leads, step by step, to a solipsism of the present moment. Anti-realists are stuck at the end of Descartes' First Meditation and are unable to transcend the radical skepticism of Hume. Quine conceded as much when he said, "I do not see that we are farther along today than where Hume left us. The Humean predicament is the human predicament."[26]

The cure for this slide into solipsism is to recognize that justification and knowledge are produced by reliable procedures such as inductive and abductive inference, and that such procedures do not cease to be reliable just because we do not have arguments to prove that they are reliable that would convince the persistent skeptic. We do not have the slightest reason to believe that our prevailing methods of justification fail to provide knowledge or approximations thereof. Moreover, we are able to confirm the reliability of every one of our prevailing methods; we are able to show that they are reliable, or that they have this or that degree of reliability, or that they are more or less reliable in this or that circumstance; and we are able to do so by applying some methods to the assessment of others. To the skeptic who protests that one is assuming that some of these methods are reliable, one should reply that the skeptic is asking for what is logically impossible—namely, to provide a proof in the absence of any method of proof. Given that we have probabilistic reasons for thinking that our theories and commonsense beliefs are true or are approximations to the truth, then we have a probabilistic basis for the ontological commitments that they entail, including belief in the reality of other minds.[27]

NATURAL SIGNS

That the demands of practical life occasionally break the bonds of epistemic restraint is not the only explanation that can be offered for our felt certainty about other minds. Thomas Reid provided another explanation in his theory of *natural signs:* "Many operations of the mind have their natural signs in the countenance, voice, and gesture."[28] A natural sign, like any other sign, represents that which it signifies to a person who understands it. What makes it natural is that it is founded upon "a connection established by nature."[29] In contrast, artificial or conventional signs are established by stipulation (as when I declare that X marks the spot) or by human action and social practices (as when spoken signs come to function as words with meaning).

How is a natural connection able to acquire the function of standing for something to someone? One way is by experience, just as we learn that smoke accompanies fire. However, Reid claims that the meanings of many gestures and facial expression cannot be learned by experience.

> When we see the sign, and see the thing signified always conjoined with it, experience may be the instructor, and teach us how that sign is to be interpreted. But how shall experience instruct us when we see the sign only, when the thing signified is invisible? Now this is the case here: the thoughts and passions of the mind, as well as the mind itself, are invisible, and therefore their connection with any sensible sign cannot be first discovered by experience; there must be some earlier source of this knowledge.[30]

Reid does not think much of the alternative that each person starts out from his own case and extrapolates what he finds to others. The reason is that our understanding of other minds emerges too early for explicit inferences to take place. Children respond to gestures, sounds, and facial expressions "almost as soon as born." "An angry countenance will fright a child in the cradle."[31] Young children have neither the time nor the ability to acquire knowledge of basic mind/body connections by experience and inference. Yet their responses to the behavior of others are often adapted to what others are feeling and thinking as these states of mind are expressed in bodily movements. The responses of very young children cannot be explained, thinks Reid, as if they were making inductive inferences, because these responses antedate the time at which children become competent in logical reasoning.

Instead, Reid proposes that the child's responses are a product of an understanding arising from "the constitution of our nature, by a kind of natural perception." It is "by our constitution, we understand the meaning of those signs, and from the sign conclude the existence of the thing signified."[32] Reid argues, "When I see the features of an expressive face, I see only figure and colour variously modified. But by the constitution of my nature, the visible object brings along with it the conception and belief of a certain passion or sentiment in the mind of the person."[33] The expression of a person in rage, for example, directly causes one who observes it to think of rage and to believe he is in rage. This belief is not a product of reasoning but, rather, a direct response to the sign.

In this way Reid distinguishes between knowledge founded upon experience and knowledge founded upon innate propensities. The meanings of some natural signs are founded upon the former and of others upon the latter. His argument can be strengthened by a remark he makes about human testimony: "Before we are capable of reasoning about testimony or authority, there are many things it concerns us to know, for which we can have no other evidence."[34] Before the child is capable of reasoning about the meaning of the behavior of others, there are many things it concerns him to know for which he has no other basis than the behavior itself, together with an inborn propensity for interpretation. In this particular case, the innate propensity consists of an ability to apply an innate concept representing a connection between a facial expression and gesture, on the one hand, and an emotion, on the other.

If such concepts are innate, they are not acquired from introspection directed upon one's own case. For Reid, our initial knowledge of the minds of others is founded upon innate knowledge of the meaning of natural signs. No doubt, experience comes into play to extend such knowledge and to refine the initial understanding founded upon innate propensities.

But what makes such beliefs cases of knowledge? That a belief is formed by an innate propensity is not sufficient to endow it with the certainty characteristic of knowledge. Again we must turn to reliabilism for an answer. Such beliefs count as knowledge to the extent that such propensities are reliable. There is an argument that makes it likely that they are reliable, namely, the point that Reid makes, as well as some Darwinians, that such beliefs are useful provided they are true.

One implication of Reid's philosophy of other minds is that the ability to exercise innate concepts and propensities antedates the capacity to use language. Some interesting consequences follow. First, it is wrong on such a theory to identify concepts with word meanings. No doubt many concepts come to be associated with words once language has been acquired, but humans possess concepts prior to speech. Second, concepts are mental representations; this means that in virtue of connecting a certain pattern of observed behavior with a certain emotion, the concept is a representation both of that behavior and of the emotion and of the fact that the former expresses the latter. Thus, there is, according to Reid's account, a great deal of innate knowledge of the human mind and of its relation to behavior.

In the third place, in virtue of being a mental representation, the concept itself is a sign, a natural sign for that matter, since it is not a product of stipulation or convention. Unlike the contingent, though natural, connection between smoke and fire and the contingent, though conventional, connection between a word and its meaning, the innate propensity to connect certain behaviors with certain emotions has this meaning because of its intrinsic or inner nature—not because of a regular connection between the concept and what it represents. It has that meaning because its having that meaning is constitutive of what it is. The concept or idea of a certain emotion and its behavioral expression represents its content intrinsically, whereas the connection between smoke and fire is extrinsic. Thus in addition to the distinction between natural and artificial signs, there is also an important distinction between intrinsic and extrinsic natural signs.

Finally, it follows from Reid's view that there is a language of thought.[35] The speech acts we form from the materials of natural language express ideas, meanings, and thoughts that can occur in the mind prior to and independently of natural language. The stream of speech expresses an inner stream of thought formulated in the medium of thought's own language. Perhaps the stream of thought is accompanied, as I speculated earlier, with a stream of brain processes so tightly connected to it that the latter is capable of functioning as the vehicle, the inner physical tokens of a brain language, expressive of the former. But that is an empirical claim yet to be verified and does not provide any reason to support the claim of naturalism that the stream of thought is reducible to the stream of brain processes.

THOUGHT AND LANGUAGE

Both Reid's theory of other minds and the view founded upon inference based upon one's own case are able to account for our knowledge of other minds, given reliabilism. However, Reid's account is certainly not immune from criticism. The most serious objection is that even if the very young child reacts appropriately to some of the gestures and facial expressions of others, such reactions consist neither of exercises of concepts nor expressions of belief; they are reflex actions. Perhaps such reflex propensities are innate, but they are automatic behavioral responses, not intellectual acts. No belief is required for reflex action. Beliefs are excluded, one might add, because there are no concepts and beliefs in the absence of language.

According to Donald Davidson, the fact that a young child or even an animal is capable of responding differentially to some of the emotions of others does not support the idea that the child possesses any concepts or beliefs at all. He bases his argument upon "*the holism of the mental.*" According to holism, "beliefs do not come one at a time: what identifies a belief and makes it the belief it is is the relationship (among other factors) to other beliefs." Moreover, thinking is not and cannot be independent of language. "What more is needed for thought? I think the answer is language."[36]

Contrary to Davidson's view, I think beliefs frequently do come one at a time. My thinking that this is yellow comes after my thinking that that is blue. Color words are learned one after the other. Holism has a better chance of being true on the theory of innate conceptual propensities, according to which a child comes into the world possessing a primitive conceptual repertoire, than on a theory that reduces concepts to word meanings that are learned sequentially. In any case, the doctrine of the holism of the mental confuses mental entities with the concepts and propositions they express. Propositions do have internal relations to one another that are essential to their identity. But the beliefs that express them do not necessarily have the same holistic unity as do propositions. For example, a proposition A may entail another B, yet a person who believes A may not believe B.

Wittgenstein also is doubtful that thought occurs independently of language. "When I think in language, there aren't 'meanings' going through my mind in addition to the verbal expressions: the language is itself the vehicle of thought."[37] Wittgenstein constructs the following thought experiment in order to challenge the idea of thought without language: "Say a sentence and think it; say it with understanding.—And now do not say it, and just do what you accompanied it with when you said it with understanding!"[38] It would appear that we do not know what to do. We do not know how to follow the instruction: think about something but do not say anything to express it either to yourself or others. The natural and perhaps the only way to think about something is to formulate your thoughts in speech. What else can one do? Thinking is just a sequence of speech acts.

But don't we often have the thoughts first and then try to express them in words? Wittgenstein acknowledges the phenomenon: "What happens when we make an effort—say in writing a letter—to find the right expression for our thoughts?—This phrase compares the process to one of translating or describing: the thoughts are already there (perhaps were there in advance) and we merely look for their expression." This phenomenon brings with it the picture of inner thought occurring independently of speech, according to which speech acts express what is in the mind independently of their verbal expression. But Wittgenstein denies that this phenomenon requires us to accept the picture. There are other ways to explain it.

> But can't all sorts of things happen here?—I surrender to a mood and the expression *comes.* Or a picture occurs to me and I try to describe it. Or an English expression occurs to me and I try to hit on the corresponding German one. Or I make a gesture, and ask myself: What words correspond to the gesture? And so on.

Such examples are intended to raise doubts in our minds about the picture of thought antecedent to language. They undermine our certainty about the presence of nonlinguistic thinking. Moreover, there are deep difficulties with the picture: "Now if it were asked: 'Do you have the thought before finding the expression?' what would one have to reply? And what, to the question: 'What did the thought consist in, as it existed before its expression?' "[39] What did it consist in? Introspection might tell us what we are thinking, but it is uninformative about the inner constitution of the acts of thinking themselves. Descartes asserted that the mind is easier to know than the body. But why, then, does this question seem so difficult to answer?

Suppose I am asked what I know about some topic, say, Leibniz's mill. Even if I have never spoken to anyone about this before, I reply with a fluent two-minute presentation expressing the core of what I know. The sequence of my speech acts is a complex series of voluntary actions under my control. It is guided by my intention to explain what I know in a manner adapted to the interests and prior knowledge of the auditor. In the light of this intention, I carefully choose the words and sentences that I utter. I recognize that most of the words in English are ambivalent, that is, they have more than one meaning. In some cases the meanings are related to one another, and in other cases they are far apart. Not only do I select the words I utter, I also select as I go along the meaning that I attach to them. I *mean* this rather than that. I choose my words carefully and deliberately to express what I want to say. Not only is there a large overall intention that guides my discourse, there are also a large number of particular intentions expressed in the choice of this word rather than that, of this meaning rather than that. This is the phenomenon of *subjective meaning.* These meanings are subjective in the sense that they are private to me, although I make them evident to others by means of what I say. If a sentence I utter is ambiguous to the auditor, I can tell him just what meaning I intended to express. My access to my own meaning is privileged, whereas the auditor depends upon my explanations for his understanding.

Objective meaning, on the other hand, is what a word means in the language. And by 'the language' I mean not just my own idiolect but what most or all speakers of the language know in virtue of knowing the language. The objective meaning of a word is the meaning reported in a good dictionary, based upon an extensive survey of its current use by speakers of the language. Each speaker draws upon objective meanings in selecting the words he uses and the meanings he chooses them to have in his efforts to communicate to others.

Objective meanings are ultimately founded upon subjective meanings. The dictionary report of objective meanings consists of statistical generalizations drawn from a sample of observed uses. What people mean is the basis for our knowledge of what the word means. Each speaker acquires his own idiolect by internalizing and sometimes modifying what others mean in his communicative interactions in early childhood. The acquisition of one's natural language depends upon identifying the subjective meanings of others as they are expressed in their speech acts and thus presupposes the ability to know what others have in mind.

In talking to someone about Leibniz's mill, I rely upon my knowledge of the semantics of words in English, as well as its syntax, in order to construct sequences of words and to select a meaning for each ambivalent expression with the intention of producing an intelligible communication. The stream of speech is guided, in addition to my understanding of the topic, by my knowledge of the language in combination with my subjective meanings. This explains why I utter these words and sentences rather than others. My subjective meaning is not itself constituted by inner speech acts couched in natural language. To insist that spoken words invariably presuppose words spoken to oneself quickly leads to an infinite regress. There is no alternative to the idea that subjective meaning is constituted by intentional states composed of intrinsic natural signs that represent what the speaker intends to say and guides his manner of saying it.

Am I saying that the stream of speech is under the complete control of the self, of the 'I' of the *Cogito*? Isn't this Humpty Dumpty's view?

> "When *I* use a word," Humpty Dumpty said, in a rather scornful tone, "it means just what I choose it to mean—neither more nor less."
>
> "The question is," said Alice, "whether you *can* make words mean different things."
>
> "The question is," said Humpty Dumpty, "which is to be master—that's all."[40]

Can one really choose to mean anything at all by a word with an established meaning? Does our mind have that degree of control over what we mean by our words? Are we really the masters of our meaning? Wittgenstein thinks not.

> Imagine someone pointing to his cheek with an expression of pain and saying "abracadabra!"—We ask "What do you mean?" And he answers "I meant toothache".—You at once think to yourself: How can one 'mean toothache' by that word? Or what did it *mean* to *mean* pain by that word? And yet, in a different context, you would have asserted that the mental activity of *meaning* such-and-such was just what was most important in using language.
>
> But can't I say "By 'abracadabra' I mean toothache"? Of course I can; but this is a definition; not a description of what goes on in me when I utter the word.[41]

Wittgenstein is calling our attention here to the fact that sometimes 'I mean X by Y' is not a report of subjective meaning but a stipulation that assigns a meaning to a word, a meaning that it did not have prior to the stipulation. Although he accepts the legitimacy of "I mean toothache by 'abracadabra,'" he doubts the truth of "I meant toothache by 'abracadabra'" interpreted as a report of "the mental activity of meaning." Perhaps he intends to deny the very existence of subjective meaning.

Wittgenstein is no doubt correct in calling our attention to the difficulty of meaning toothache by 'abracadabra', just as Alice is puzzled by Humpty Dumpty's meaning 'a nice knock-down argument' by 'glory'. What is puzzling is that in both cases the speaker is using words in a way that has no semantic connection to their standard uses and the established habits of speakers of the language—while at the same time attempting to communicate with those who have nothing else to rely upon except the standard uses. This is a kind of pragmatic inconsistency. The desire to communicate, together with the need to make use of what the auditors can be expected to know, places severe constraints upon subjective meaning. Deviations from established usage are usually met by incomprehension, although, in some cases, as with Mrs. Malaprop or poetic metaphor, the context allows us to hit upon the correct interpretation. Yes, one is master of one's meaning, but even a master must conform to established usage if he is to succeed in being understood by others.

Chapter Three

SELF-CONSCIOUSNESS AND THOUGHT

DESCARTES' *COGITO* AS AN IMMEDIATE INFERENCE

In this chapter I shall discuss introspective knowledge of our thoughts, a major example of representational consciousness. I shall start with the ideas centering about Descartes' *Cogito* that were introduced in chapter 1. Having found reasons to doubt almost all the things he formerly believed, Descartes was able to prove 'I exist' because the very effort to doubt 'I exist' entails 'I exist'. From that he inferred that it was his nature or essence to be a thinking thing, a thing that thinks, doubts, imagines, dreams, perceives, wills, and so forth.

A proof requires one or more premises. For Descartes, one of the premises used to establish 'I exist' is either 'I think' or, for that matter, any proposition that reports an instance of thinking. Is that sufficient for his proof? Are any other premises required? One suggestion that had been offered is that his proof is really a syllogism whose major premise is 'Everything that thinks exists'. But Descartes rejected this suggestion out of hand:

> And when we become aware that we are thinking things, this is a primary notion which is not derived by means of any syllogism. When someone says 'I am thinking, therefore I am, or I exist,' he does not deduce existence from thought by means of a syllogism, but recognizes it as something

> self-evident by a simple intuition of the mind. This is clear from the fact that if he were deducing it by means of a syllogism, he would have to have had previous knowledge of the major premiss 'Everything which thinks is, or exists'; yet in fact he learns it from experiencing in his own case that it is impossible that he should think without existing. It is in the nature of our mind to construct general propositions on the basis of our knowledge of particular ones.[1]

'I think, therefore I exist' is a self-evident truth apprehended by "a simple intuition of the mind." If we should think of it as a proof arrived at by means of an inference, it is of the kind that Aristotelian logic called an immediate inference—a conclusion based upon a single premise, not a syllogism at all. 'I exist' follows directly from 'I think' without the need of a major premise to guarantee the connection.

KNOWLEDGE OF THE UNIVERSAL

In fact, rather than one's knowledge of the *Cogito* depending upon a syllogism containing a major premise, the general proposition 'Everything which thinks is, or exists' is known through the particular. Such knowledge cannot be generated as an induction from various instances because, in the circumstances in which it is accessible to Descartes, he is confined to only one instance. He is limited to that one instance and what follows logically and conceptually from it. Two facts are of the essence here. First, according to Descartes, "it is impossible that he should think without existing." His thinking *entails* his existing. Second, the necessary connection between 'I think' and 'I exist' does not depend upon the identity of the person who is thinking. In this case, the person happens to be Descartes himself, but it could be anyone else for that matter. Who is doing the thinking is irrelevant. Take anyone you like, if that person thinks, then that person exists. Although the *Meditations* is written in the first person and refers only to Descartes, when he later comes to explain his proof, as in the passage quoted in the previous section, he recognizes that anyone who thinks can similarly prove that he exists.

Moreover, it is not essential as far as the deduction of existence is concerned that the verb in the premise represents a type of thinking. Any action will serve to establish existence because only an existing thing can act. The only reason that thinking plays an indispensable role in Descartes' proof is epistemic—thinking is the only sort of action he can know about after doubting everything else.

For this reason, the truth of 'Everything which thinks is, or exists' can be proved on the basis of 'I think, therefore, I exist'. A simple intuition of the mind grasps the connection between 'I think' and 'I exist'. Reflection upon the connection reveals that the identity of the person is irrelevant for 'I think' to entail 'I exist'. The connection holds no matter who is thinking, a fact equivalent to 'Everything which thinks is, or exists'. The transition from knowledge of the particular to knowledge of the universal is founded upon the very same intuition that yields knowledge of the particular when that intuition is supplemented by a realization of the irrelevance of the identity of the thinker. This insight is accessible from within the intuition itself.

THE TRANSITION FROM 'I THINK' TO 'I EXIST'

Descartes has provided a name—"a simple intuition of the mind"—to the mental act that directly apprehends the necessary connection between a person's acts and the existence of the actor. Because the inference is immediate, it is not founded upon any further reasoning, and, therefore, the knowledge of the connection is self-evident, that is, evident through itself rather than through something else as in a syllogism or induction. It becomes evident to the one who is thinking not by any considerations external to itself but by the transparency of the connection.

Although Descartes does not clearly explain the nature of the connection that makes it both necessary and self-evident, I would like to suggest what such an explanation might be. Consider going through the *Cogito* argument yourself. When you put yourself in Descartes' place at the end of the First Meditation, you have suspended any knowledge you might think you have of facts about your own identity. You do not know your name, your occupation, your country, your place of birth, or your current circumstances. The only fact accessible to you is the fact that you yourself are thinking. That is why it is essential that the premise 'I think' be couched in the first-person singular. For it is only in this way that the thinker knows how to refer to himself. He knows nothing else, no name or description that designates him impersonally as the one who is thinking. All his characterizations of his own acts of thought must be formulated in the first person.

Consider now Descartes' thinking about whether or not he himself exists. There are many ways in which *we* can describe his thinking: "Descartes is thinking," "The author of the *Meditations* is thinking," and so forth. All of these descriptions may very well be accurate. But Descartes himself is confined to the first person in characterizing his own acts of thought. Any assertion that he might make—to himself or to others if there are any others in the vicinity—must employ the first person. Consider now the assertion he makes when he says, "I am thinking about whether or not I exist." Such an assertion as an act of Descartes must employ the first-person singular pronoun in some language or other, either in a natural language or in a brain language or a mental language, if there are such things.

A necessary condition for this assertion to be true is that there exists someone who is thinking that thought, and that someone is the one named by the first-person pronoun used in the assertion. That it is a necessary condition is grasped through our understanding of just what that assertion says. Such understanding is gained through our knowledge of the meaning of the sentence used in making that assertion. We understand that 'thinking' denotes a kind of action that could not occur unless there exists an agent doing it, where the agent in question is the one designated by 'I'.

Thus the simple intuition of the mind that verifies the truth of 'I think, therefore, I exist', that shows that 'I exist' necessarily follows from 'I think', recognizes that a truth condition of 'I think' is logically sufficient for the truth of 'I exist'. If we think of supplying truth conditions as a way of explaining the meaning of an assertion, then we can say that the *Cogito* is or appears to be true in virtue of its meaning. Does that mean that it is an analytic statement? Not exactly. There is more to the story than this.

We must keep in mind that Descartes intends the *Cogito* to constitute a proof of 'I exist'. But there are various sorts of proof, and these can be classified in different ways. The classification that I have in mind is between proofs that are hypothetical and those that are categorical. In a *hypothetical proof,* the conclusion follows from the premise. Such a proof amounts to this: if the premise is true, then necessarily the conclusion is true as well. Taken hypothetically, the *Cogito* amounts to the statement: If it is true that I am thinking, then necessarily it is true that I exist. Since the consequent expresses part of the content of the antecedent, the hypothetical statement is analytic and so is the associated inference.

A *categorical proof* proves the truth of the conclusion; it allows us to detach the conclusion from the premise and to assert it in its own right. The premise is put forward, not hypothetically as a proposition to be entertained, but as true. Clearly Descartes intends the *Cogito* to be categorical. He claims to have brought his doubts to an end by asserting 'I think' and recognizing through a simple intuition of the mind that 'I exist' must be true as well.

Taken categorically, the *Cogito* resists an interpretation in terms of the semantic category of analyticity. Although its inferential transition is analytic, nevertheless, both premise and conclusion are separately asserted, and these are contingent claims whose truth is based not merely on semantic facts but also on the facts that Descartes is thinking and that Descartes exists.

Two sorts of categorical proofs need to be distinguished. Some categorical proofs are *sound;* in these, not only does the conclusion follow validly from the premise, but the premise is true as well. A sound categorical proof establishes that the conclusion is true. An *epistemically sound proof* is not only valid and sound but also provides knowledge of the truth of the conclusion. In order for a person to gain knowledge of the truth of the conclusion by means of a proof, he would have to know both that the premise is true and that the conclusion follows from the premise. In that case he would know that the conclusion is true and would be entitled to assert it.

Is the *Cogito* epistemically sound? To answer this question, one would first have to determine whether or not Descartes is able to overcome the skeptical arguments of the First Meditation. Since I have already dealt with skepticism in general, I will confine my remarks to the problem of self-knowledge. Does Descartes actually know the truth of the premise 'I think'?

THE PROBLEM OF SELF-KNOWLEDGE: TRANSPARENCY OF THE SELF

The 'I think' is an act of the self. Knowledge of the 'I think' has two components: the content of the thinking or the proposition asserted in the act of thinking is one, and the other is the self that is doing the thinking. The question of self-knowledge concerns our cognitive access to both. In this section, I shall confine myself to a remark in which Descartes undertakes to explain how he knows the 'I think'.

In replying to an objection from Antoine Arnauld, Descartes asserts: "As to the fact that there can be nothing in the mind, in so far as it is a thinking thing, of which it is not aware, this seems to me to be self-evident. . . . We cannot have any thought of which we are not aware at the very moment when it is in us. . . . we are always actually aware of the acts or operations of our minds."[2] In this passage, Descartes asserts a restricted *principle of the transparency of thinking* (PTT), according to which a person is aware of his thoughts simultaneously with his thinking them.

How shall we understand the notion of awareness that Descartes employs? One alternative is to think of introspective awareness simply as the direct and immediate knowledge of one's act of thought. I am, for example, thinking about eating the apple on the table, and so I immediately and directly know that I am thinking about eating it. This interpretation, however, generates an infinite regress; my knowledge of my thinking is another case of thinking of which one has knowledge, and so on *ad infinitum.* (See the section "Consciousness" in chapter 1.) But we find no such infinity of simultaneous distinct acts of thought, so this interpretation is unacceptable.

Another alternative is to interpret introspective awareness by analogy with sense perception. I see the apple on the table, and, by this means, I learn that there is one there. Visual observation is the basis of my knowledge of this matter of fact. In introspection, there is something analogous to observation by means of the senses. This is the view later adopted by Locke when he defined introspection (or reflection, in his terms) as "the *perception of the operations of our own minds*" and stated that "though it be not sense, as having nothing to do with external objects, yet it is very like it, and might properly enough be called internal sense."[3] The analogy with sense thwarts the infinite regress. Although I see the apple when it occupies a portion of my field of vision, yet through inattention or other reasons, I may fail to notice it and fail to gain knowledge of it. In the same way, introspective observation may not be followed by introspective knowledge. Observational awareness does not entail representational awareness. Although this interpretation is not refuted by the implication of an infinite regress, it is implausible for a different reason. In perceptual observation, the object that is seen appears or looks to the observer in some way. Sense perception consists in the appearance of objects by means of the stimulation of the senses. However, in introspection, we do not find anything analogous to sensory appearances. There is nothing analogous to a sensation that corresponds to an act of thinking. The analogy with sensory observation is simply mistaken.

Descartes has occasionally been criticized for denying the existence of unconscious thinking. For example, Peirce objects that Descartes "is taking it for granted that nothing in his nature lies hidden beneath the surface."[4] However, Peirce exaggerates. After all, PTT applies only to current acts of thought. These may be forgotten and in that sense become unconscious. They may be not only forgotten but also repressed and inaccessible to ordinary self-reflection. Though repressed, their traces may still be active and thus constitute a dynamic unconscious in Freud's sense.[5] All this is compatible with PTT.

In his reply to Arnauld, Descartes claims that PTT is self-evident. That is difficult to accept. It is not clear what there is about the nature of thinking that makes it transparent. Why should the occurrence of a thought necessitate the occurrence of knowledge of it or awareness of it? PTT is certainly not analytic. On the contrary, it is self-evident that a thought can occur without any accompanying knowledge of it.

In any case, that we have knowledge of some of our thoughts is undeniable. It is also undeniable that we do not know how we know what we are thinking. If there are any brain or mental mechanisms that make self-consciousness possible, we do not yet know what they are. If you ask me how I know that I am thinking about the apple on the table, my answer is:

I have no idea. One should not pretend to know what one does not know. However, the rejection of PTT does not provide any reason for thinking that Descartes does not know the truth of 'I think'. The existence of a fact is not called into question by the absence of any known explanation of that fact.

KNOWLEDGE OF THE THINKER

One of the mental assertions capable of standing as a premise of the *Cogito* is 'I doubt that I exist'. By means of introspective awareness, Descartes would be capable of coming to know that what he is thinking is doubting that he exists; by an intuition of the mind, he would also know that doubting is a type of thinking and that this thinking is an action performed by a certain agent; he would also know that the agent in question is the one designated by 'I' in his assertion and that the one so designated is himself. His knowledge of who is doing the thinking is not simply a consciousness of a self; it is self-consciousness, a knowledge that he himself is thinking.

For Descartes, the self is a substance, a category derived from the Aristotelian metaphysical tradition but which also has a foundation in the commonsense distinction between a thing and its properties or attributes. A thing or substance is something that has or exemplifies properties; not being itself a property, it is incapable of being exemplified by anything else. It is a subject of predicates that is not itself a predicate. If a substance is also an *active agent,* such as a person or God, then it is capable not only of being influenced by the actions of other things, but also of initiating actions in its own right; it has free will. It acts, though it is not itself an act.

Descartes accepts the established view that one gains knowledge of a substance only through knowledge of its discernible properties or attributes, including its actions. For example, I know that this is an apple by seeing its color, shape, and size, by feeling how hard it is, by tasting its taste, and so on. Its properties tell me what type of substance it is and also individuate it as an instance of that type. In general, says Descartes, "we do not have immediate knowledge of substances. . . . We know them only by perceiving certain forms or attributes which must inhere in something if they are to exist."[6] Although we are "aware of the acts and operations of our own minds," we lack direct awareness of the substance that exemplifies them. How then do we verify the existence of the 'I' in 'I think'? Descartes answers: "It is certain that a thought cannot exist without a thing that is thinking; and in general no act or accident can exist without a substance for it to belong to. But we do not come to know a substance immediately, through being aware of the substance itself; we come to know it only through its being the subject of certain acts."[7] We are never aware of the substance itself; we have no direct knowledge of it. Lodged in our minds is a general principle that automatically leads us to infer the existence of the substance through being aware of some of its attributes. Call it the *substance/attribute principle* (SAP): "No act or accident can exist without a substance for it to belong to."

Descartes' knowledge within the *Cogito* that someone is thinking is gained by the cooperation of introspective awareness and SAP. The former tells him that thinking is going on. The latter tells him that where thinking is going on, there is a substance that is engaged in that very thinking. One must suppose that there is a mental mechanism that activates SAP when a person is confronted with a bundle of properties.

But what reason does Descartes have for thinking that SAP is true? At the stage of his argument in which he enunciates the *Cogito,* he would have no option except to claim that it is self-evident. It is in the very nature of an attribute to be exemplified by something, and where that attribute is an act of thought, it is in its very nature for it to be exemplified by a thinking substance.

THE PROBLEM OF SELF-CONSCIOUSNESS

I intend now to consider two lines of criticism that may be directed against Descartes' efforts to solve the problem of self-knowledge. The first one is willing to concede that SAP is true, and, therefore, that the inference from the proposition that thinking is going on to the conclusion that there exists a thinker producing this thought is sound. According to this view, Descartes has succeeded in proving the existence of a thinking thing. However, the *Cogito* asserts not merely that some thinker exists but that the thinker is oneself, the very person engaged in the *Cogito.* In thinking the *Cogito,* one is proving the existence not just of some thinker or other but of oneself.

The *Cogito* is an instance of self-consciousness. Descartes uses the term 'I' to designate himself. Yet SAP is incapable of justifying an inference to himself or to any identified thinker. Of course, it does justify an inference to some particular thinker, namely, to the one doing that thinking. But it does not identify who that thinker is, and, in particular, it does not tell us that the thinker is oneself. As an abstract metaphysical rule, SAP permits one to infer the existence of a substance that exemplifies any property of which one is conscious. But it does not tell us which substance it is nor does it validate that special sense of self implied in self-consciousness.

If he had recognized the problem, Descartes might have introduced the following *principle of self-consciousness* (PSC): Whenever one is directly aware of an act of thinking, then it is one's own thinking one is aware of. According to PSC, Descartes would be entitled to infer from his direct awareness of an act of thinking that he is the one that is thinking. He would be entitled to go from the premise 'Thinking is going on', verified directly, to 'I think' and from thence to 'I exist'. SAP could then be bypassed entirely as far as the *Cogito* is concerned, only later to be introduced in order to establish the existence of material substances.

One might be inclined to believe that SAP is self-evident while wondering whether the same status could be ascribed to PSC. Questions arise as to the extent of the direct awareness of attributes. Am I directly aware of the red color of the apple? The tendency in Descartes is to restrict direct awareness to the contents of one's own mind. Perhaps there is a *principle of direct awareness* (PDA) at work here, according to which anything a person is directly aware of is a property or attribute of his own mind. But is this self-evident? Isn't the inclination to accept it the product of a complex and controversial series of arguments used to support the representational theory of mind? Isn't it a conclusion rather than a candidate for a self-evident premise? These worries about PDA lead me to believe that Descartes' *Cogito* fails to overcome the powerful skeptical arguments that he must overthrow in order to establish the certainty that is his goal. It is not that the *Cogito* is false, although we do not yet understand how it is possible to know that it is true. Rather, the point is that Descartes' quest for certainty collapses because of his failure to justify bringing himself into the story.

But there is a more significant problem here than Descartes' inability to justify certain principles of inference. Even if he could overcome these problems of justification and establish through self-evident principles that he himself is the thinker who exists, this solution misconceives the problem of self-consciousness. For a person's use of 'I' to assert something of himself is not founded upon inference at all. In self-consciousness, a person achieves a direct and intimate connection to himself that is not mediated by abstract principles of inference. A person does not have the sense that his self-understanding, his ability to use 'I' to refer to himself, rests upon a controversial process of reasoning. One does not first become aware of some contents bereft of the 'I' and then, with the help of metaphysical reasoning, infer that these contents are such that the 'I' is what exemplifies them; rather, the 'I' travels with the contents as their intimate companion. There is something mistaken in the idea, certainly not confined to Descartes' philosophy, that one's knowledge of substances is and can only be inferential.

In a remarkable passage, Nietzsche denies that there is non-inferential knowledge of oneself:

> When I analyze the process that is expressed in the sentence, "I think," I find a whole series of daring assertions that would be difficult, perhaps impossible, to prove; for example, that it is *I* who think, that there must necessarily be something that thinks, that thinking is an activity and operation on the part of a being who is thought of as a cause, that there is an "ego," and finally, that it is already determined what is to be designated by thinking—that I *know* what thinking is. For if I had not already decided within myself what it is, by what standard could I determine whether that which is just happening is not perhaps "willing" or "feeling"? In short, the assertion "I think" assumes that I *compare* my state at the present moment with other states of myself which I know, in order to determine what it is; on account of this retrospective connection with further "knowledge," it has, at any rate, no immediate certainty for me.[8]

Later in this chapter I shall consider Nietzsche's doubts about the reality of the ego or mental substance, but here I focus upon his claim about self-knowledge. Nietzsche argues here that the only way one is able to determine the nature of one's current mental state is by comparing it to previous states; if it resembles a previous act of will, for example, then one is entitled to claim that this one is an act of will as well. For Nietzsche, a shaky inference founded upon a fallible comparison is enough to undermine any claim to certainty in reports of one's mental life.

Nietzsche fails to note, however, that the same problem arises in the identification of the previous states of mind. How do I know that that one was an act of will? Presumably another act of comparison is required that takes one back further into the past. It looks as if Nietzsche's account leads to a regress that has no end. There is no particular reason to restrict it to states of mind. My ability to judge that this table is rectangular also, if he is correct, presupposes a comparison of its shape with shapes perceived in the past. Again an unending regress is generated. Without intending it, Nietzsche's argument leads not only to a rejection of immediate certainty in the identification of one's own states of mind, but to a general skepticism directed at the ascription of any predicate to any object whatever.

There is an alternative account of predication that does not generate an unending regress of conditions. One is able to apply predicates such as 'rectangular' to an object or 'act of will' to a state of mind in virtue of knowing their meaning. Because one knows what 'rectangular' means, one knows what shape it designates and one knows how to recognize it. Once a person has attained the *conceptual knowledge* incorporated in the meaning of a predicate, he no longer needs to rely upon previous instances in order to apply it to this instance. No doubt, one's acquisition of an instance of conceptual knowledge depends upon one's experience of the application of the predicate to objects and events by people in one's speech community. In the absence of such experiences, one would have no idea which property constitutes the concept associated with a given empirical predicate. No doubt we lack even a partial understanding of the mental and physical mechanisms that explain how conceptual knowledge is possible. But one does not need such an explanation in order to be sure that one does indeed have the conceptual knowledge associated with a predicate. Correct usage is the standard we use to tell that a person knows the meaning of a word; it does not matter how he acquired that skill. Nietzsche illegitimately incorporates a dubious account of the conditions necessary for the correct application of a predicate into a description of the standards of correct usage.

SUBSTANCE AND THE SELF

Another objection to Descartes' understanding of self-knowledge is founded upon empiricist arguments directed against the very notion of substance. If a substance is that which possesses attributes, although not itself an attribute, we might attempt to discover more about the nature of any particular substance by abstracting in thought from all the attributes in order to reveal the substance in its bare nakedness. However, there is nothing to reveal, since its entire content is contained in its discernable attributes; there is nothing there to be known. What is left after the process of abstraction is completed is a bare particular or a featureless prime matter or an unknown substratum whose only function is to exemplify attributes. But, says the empiricist, if it lacks all content, it is indistinguishable from nothing. In fact, it is nothing.

This critique of the traditional concept of substance begins with Locke and Berkeley and culminates in this passage from Hume's *Treatise*:

> If it [the idea of substance] be convey'd to us by our senses, I ask, which of them; and after what manner? If it be perceiv'd by the eyes, it must be a colour; if by the ears, a sound; if by the palate, a taste; and so of the other senses. But I believe none will assert, that substance is either a colour, or a sound, or a taste. The idea of substance must therefore be deriv'd from an impression of reflexion, if it really exist. But the impressions of reflexion resolve themselves into our passions and emotions; none of which can possibly represent a substance. We have therefore no idea of substance, distinct from that of a collection of particular qualities, nor have we any other meaning when we either talk or reason concerning it.[9]

Here Hume rejects by implication the metaphysics of SAP. Qualities can stand alone; they need no separate particulars to exemplify them. The concept of substance survives in Hume in an attenuated form as a bundle of particularized qualities. To say, for example, that this apple is red simply means that a particular instance of a shade of red is a member of the bundle that we designate by the term 'this apple'. Exemplification turns into the relation between a quality and the bundle of which it is a member.

In a famous passage, Hume applies his general critique of substance to the special case of the self:

> For my part, when I enter most intimately into what I call *myself,* I always stumble upon some particular perception or other, of heat or cold, light or shade, love or hatred, pain or pleasure. I never can catch *myself* at any time without a perception, and never can observe any thing but the perception. . . . [Individual persons] are nothing but a bundle or collection of different perceptions, which succeed each other with an inconceivable rapidity, and are in a perpetual flux and movement. . . . The mind is a kind of theatre, where several perceptions successively make their appearance: pass, re-pass, glide away, and mingle in an infinite variety of postures and situations.[10]

The stream of consciousness, then, is all there is to the self. Any distinguishable item in the stream, whether a sense impression, a thought, or an emotion, can exist by itself, needing no separate substance to exemplify it.

It may be of interest to note that Hume's rejection of a substantial self in favor of a flowing stream of consciousness was anticipated two thousand years earlier in Buddhism's denial of the ego or inner self:

> Just as the word 'chariot' is but a mode of expression for axle, wheels, chariot-body, pole, and other constituent members in a certain relation to each other, but when we come to examine the members one by one, we discover in the absolute sense there is no chariot; . . . in exactly the same way the words 'living entity' and 'Ego' are but a mode of expression for the presence of the five attachment groups, but when we come to examine the elements of being one by one, we discover that in the absolute sense there is no living entity to form a basis for such figments as 'I am' or 'I'.[11]

This denial of the ego is not merely an abstract metaphysical thesis but has implications for the way life should be lived. A hint of the broader understanding of the right way of life is expressed in this passage: "Misery only doth exist, none miserable. No doer is there; naught save the deed is found. Nirvana is, but not the man who seeks it. The path exists, but not the traveler on it."[12]

THE RETURN OF THE EGO

It is difficult to sustain a consistent denial of the substantial self: *Who* is it who denies it? I am reminded of the philosopher who once claimed that solipsism is such a plausible theory that it is surprising that there are not more solipsists. In saying "I can never catch myself without a perception, and never can observe anything but a perception," Hume appears to reinstate the very self he had reduced to a mere bundle. What can this 'I' be that is looking for itself, that can never find itself, and that can observe the passing constituents of its own stream of consciousness? The self is elusive, no doubt. The traveler on the path can see the path but not himself traversing it. The attempt to cast doubt upon the reality of the traveler, however, presupposes his very existence in the reference to a path being traversed. Every attempt to catch the self through introspective awareness pushes it into the background as the agent attending to something else. But can there be a foreground without a background?

The Buddhist disciple "conceives an aversion for consciousness": "And in conceiving this aversion he becomes divested of passion, and by the absence of passion he becomes free, and when he is free he becomes aware that he is free."[13] Who is the self that is able to divest himself of the very stream of consciousness that is supposed to constitute his very self? The language in which we attempt to raise skeptical doubts about the substantial self presupposes the very thing being doubted. It is difficult to shake off Descartes' *Cogito* argument.

In *The Principles of Psychology,* William James claims that if psychology is to count as an empirical science, it must reject the Cartesian metaphysics of a separate substantial self. To the extent that psychology is concerned with "a man's inner or subjective being," it must confine attention to the empirically given "stream of our personal consciousness, or the present 'segment' or 'section' of the stream, according as we take a broader or narrower view—both the stream and the section being concrete existences in time, and each being a unity after its own peculiar kind."[14]

James attempts to solve the very problem that stumped Hume, namely, how to understand the unity of the stream. If the self is an aggregate or bundle of elements, what is the basis for assigning any given element to a determinate bundle? Take a sensation S that occurs at a certain time. Is it a sensation that Peter feels or one that Paul feels? How can we assign S to Peter rather than Paul or to Paul rather than Peter? James claims that "the breach from one mind to another is perhaps the greatest breach in nature." How is it that Peter and Paul are never in doubt about which elements of the stream belong to which of them?

> When Paul and Peter wake up in the same bed, and recognize that they have been asleep, each one of them mentally reaches back and makes connection with but *one* of the two streams of thought which were broken by the sleeping hours. . . . Peter's present instantly finds out Peter's past, and never by mistake knits itself on to that of Paul. Paul's thought in turn is as little liable to go astray. The past thought of Peter is appropriated by the present Peter alone.[15]

How do Peter and Paul manage to do it? It does not seem that any of the relations among the elements are sufficient as criteria for the unity of the self. Resemblance cannot be a criterion, for Peter's sensation may resemble Paul's, and yet neither is in doubt about which belongs to which. Causality cannot be a criterion, because a thought in Peter's mind may initiate a chain of events that terminates with a thought in Paul's mind. Contiguity cannot be a criterion, because sleep and unconsciousness produce breaks in the stream of consciousness.

In some contexts, James relies upon a peculiar feeling as the basis for unity: "If the thinking be *our* thinking, it must be suffused through all its parts with that peculiar warmth and intimacy that make it come as ours."[16] Reliance upon such metaphors, however, cannot be the basis for an explanation of the unity of consciousness. The basic fact about the unity of consciousness is that for each person, there are a large number of past and present mental states which he *knows* are *his.* How that is accomplished is one of those mysteries about which we know nothing.

But if, as James insists, the requirements of a scientific psychology prevent us from relying upon a substantial self in our theorizing, how shall we understand the phenomenon of self-consciousness? What is the self that knows which items belong to its own stream? James suggests the following answer:

> This me is an empirical aggregate of things objectively known. The I which knows them cannot itself be an aggregate, neither for psychological purposes need it be considered to be an unchanging metaphysical entity like the Soul, or a principle like the pure Ego, viewed as 'out of time'. It is a *Thought,* at each moment different from that of the last moment, but *appropriative* of the latter, together with all that the latter called its own. All the experiential facts find their place in this description, unencumbered with any hypothesis save that of the existence of passing thoughts or states of mind.[17]

According to James, the thing that knows the elements that belong to its own stream of thoughts and knows that they are elements in its stream of thoughts is itself one of these very thoughts. A given thought in some way appropriates other thoughts and knows them as its own.

Although James attempts to do without a substantial self, he finds that he needs something to perform the function of self-consciousness that the Cartesian tradition had ascribed to mental substances. His solution simply reifies thoughts; it ascribes to them the traditional functions of substantial selves, namely, knowing their own states of mind. In fact, what James does is to turn each member of the stream of thoughts into a substantial self capable of action and knowledge, of appropriation and self-consciousness. He does not actually do without a substantial self; he multiplies them without limit. But then the self of everyday life simply disappears from view, and in its place is a series of momentary selves each passing its sense of identity to future members of the series. But do not the very same problems arise for each of these momentary selves as arose for the substantial self of Descartes? How does it interact with the brain? What is the stuff of which it is composed? How does it intermingle with the body? How does it connect to the other momentary selves to constitute the unity of a person? It looks as if the attempt to replace the substantial self with a bundle of perceptions or a stream of thoughts, while ascribing to the latter the same functions as were ascribed to the former, accomplishes nothing of philosophical value. James' assumption that generates such paradoxical conclusions is his insistence that psychology is an empirical science and hence must not introduce entities incapable of empirical confirmation. But perhaps James adopts a notion of empirical confirmation that is too constrained and fails to conform to the scientific methodology that he endorses.

IS THE SELF AN ILLUSION?

Georg Christoph Lichtenberg once remarked that instead of saying 'I think', one should say 'It thinks', where 'it' has the same use as in 'It rains'.[18] We understand that the 'it' in 'It rains' is non-referential and merely functions to fill a subject place for a predicate to latch onto. Similarly, we should understand the 'I' in 'I think' as non-referential; therefore, it is a fallacy to apply existential generalization to the 'I think', for doing so mistakenly supposes that 'I' designates a real underlying subject.

Some philosophers have gone so far as to indict the subject-predicate syntax of language as fostering ways of thinking that encourage the illusion of there being permanent substantial realities transcending the flux of experience. Thus Whitehead recommends "the abandonment of the subject-predicate forms of thought, so far as concerns the presupposition that this form is a direct embodiment of the ultimate characterization of fact. The result is that the 'substance-quality' concept is avoided; and that morphological description is replaced by description of dynamic process."[19] Whitehead is indebted here to William James' view of the self as a process whose elements inherit unifying characteristics from the past and transmit them to the future. The whole idea is a development of Hume's bundle theory, but we have seen that it contains intractable difficulties.

Nietzsche develops Lichtenberg's remark in the following profound passage:

> A thought comes when "it" wishes, and not when "I" wish, so that it is a falsification of the facts of the case to say that the subject "I" is the con-

> dition of the predicate "think." *It* thinks; but that this "it" is precisely the famous old "ego" is, to put it mildly, only a supposition, an assertion, and assuredly not an "immediate certainty." After all, one has even gone too far with this "it thinks"—even the "it" contains an *interpretation* of the process, and does not belong to the process itself. One infers here according to grammatical habit: "Thinking is an activity; every activity requires an agent; consequently—."[20]

Nietzsche, like Hume, challenges Descartes' SAP. Mental activities do not require an underlying active agent. No ego is required for the existence of thinking. Nietzsche claims that our grammatical habits impose an interpretation upon the stream of thought, making it appear that the old ego is indispensable. The 'I' in 'I think' is not a genuine referring expression at all, at least not an expression that permits existential quantification; it is merely a placeholder that functions to fill an empty grammatical space. The 'I' is a requirement of syntax only and implies no ontological commitments.

But there are problems with Nietzsche's disavowal of the old ego. It is true that we frequently find that a thought occurs to us without any conscious activity on our part. But that is far from the whole story. Just as often, thinking is a self-controlled process in which we consciously deliberate about some intellectual or practical problem we want to solve. Take a trivial case: I am looking for my watch. Where did I put it? I try to remember the various places in my house or my neighborhood where I might have left it. I estimate certain probabilities of its being here rather than there. I conclude that it is most probably there, and I go to find it. Throughout this process, it has been the same 'I' examining this possibility and that possibility, making this estimate and that estimate, and finally coming to a conclusion and deciding to act in the light of the conclusion. Of course, any example of self-controlled thought incorporates functions whose underlying neural mechanisms one does not know at all. How have these memories been stored? How am I able to bring them to consciousness? What accounts for the accuracy of my probability estimates? I have no understanding how all this is accomplished. Neither does anyone else. Yet some parts of the process are under my control. Moreover, the person who wondered where his watch is and who engaged in these voluntary deliberations and who came to this conclusion and acted in this way is the same person throughout the process. This is a truth that is a datum to be dealt with, not an illusion to be dismissed.

Lichtenberg is correct in his remark that in 'It rains', 'it' is an empty non-referential placeholder. A consequence of this fact is that one cannot validly infer from 'It rains' the conclusion that there exists something that rains. 'It rains' entails that raining is going on, and this is an event that does not presuppose an active agent. We understand this because we know what raining is, and we know that raining, as well as many other events, does not have this presupposition. We are not at the mercy of grammatical habits; our understanding of the nature of the facts represented allows us to suppress the inference to a metaphysical subject. In fact, because of this understanding, we have no inclination to make such an inference at all. Our understanding of our categories of interpretation makes us realize that to infer a metaphysical subject from 'It rains' would be a category mistake.

But there is no analogous category mistake in inferring that there is something that thinks from 'I think'. Such an inference does not generate a sense of linguistic absurdity, as does the one from 'It rains'. The fact that we recognize that there is a category mistake in the one case but not in the other demonstrates that we are not at the mercy of syntax. The idea that the subject-predicate grammar imposes a metaphysical interpretation upon us is an exaggeration. We bring our semantics or understanding of meaning to legitimize the consciousness of a thinker from the existence of thinking. Our grasp of the meaning of the 'I think' is an insight into the sort of thing that thinking is, and, in particular, that it is an activity that presupposes an active agent.

The case of 'It rains' shows that not every term that occurs in the predicate position designates an attribute that presupposes the existence of something that exemplifies it. Verbs sometimes designate events with no implication of exemplification. Subject to this restriction, our categorial understanding of the nature of attributes, substances, and exemplification incorporates SAP. Such an understanding is the basis for our endorsing the truth of many assertions, such as the fact that I am the same person who first was looking for my watch and later found it. However, even if SAP should be true in this restricted sense, it is not necessary in order to establish the existence of the 'I' in the *Cogito.* This is another example of the universal being known through the particular. Because I grasp that this act of thinking, simply because it is an act of thinking, presupposes the existence of an active agent, I am in a position to endorse the restricted version of SAP.

Perhaps Lichtenberg, Nietzsche, James, and Whitehead would agree that our prevailing categorial system justifies us in accepting the old ego, but, they might insist, that merely shows that the prevailing system is mistaken; it is a collection of prejudices that must be revised or even replaced by a new system that respects empiricist and scientific requirements. Away with the old metaphysics, no matter how deeply entrenched it is in our ordinary modes of thought.

The problem with this way of dispensing with the old ego is that it is incompatible with many things that we know to be true. It is incompatible with all the beliefs we have about the identity of persons through time. It is not true that the prevailing system incorporates out-of-date habits of thought that deserve to be swept away. These are not merely habits but true assertions, and whatever contradicts the truth is false.

Of course, when I state that these are true assertions, I am implying that I take them to be true, and one can easily reply that, whatever I think, they are not really true. I do not intend to defend all the modes of thought that prevail in our intellectual and practical life. The fact that a mode of thought prevails and has prevailed for millennia is not a conclusive guarantee of truth, although it is a reason for holding onto it until something better comes along. But if one undertakes to overturn a prevailing, deeply entrenched way of thinking about the world and the self, one had better have excellent reasons to explain how it is possible that the beliefs that we thought are true really are not and to show that the new system is superior to the old.

The basic argument against the prevailing system is the one that Hume and James endorsed, namely, that the old ego cannot be supported by experience. This is an argument to be taken seriously, but in the hands of Hume and James it assumes a narrow view of what experience is capable of supporting. Basically, what Hume and James claim is that we cannot find the old ego by introspection. Look carefully, and you won't find it, so there is no such thing. This way of arguing, however, overlooks the fact that the existence of entities that cannot be found directly by sense perception or introspection may be established through insight or abductive inference, conceptual analysis, and other modes of theorizing. Modern science, as well as ordinary thought, is committed to the existence of numerous entities that are not directly accessible to our cognitive system.

The writings of Hume and James suggest another way of looking at the matter that is consistent with prevailing habits of thought. They suggest that the old ego is, to use a phrase introduced by Bertrand Russell, a logical construction out of entities given in experience. Thus, the old ego is just a bundle of perceptions or stream of thoughts. However, we have seen that these constructive endeavors have ended in failure. The only adequate explanation of the unity of the bundle or of the stream is that its elements belong to the same person. The person is conceptually prior to his experiences; his experiences are individuated by the fact that they belong to him.

THE EVIDENCE FROM NEUROSCIENCE.

Everybody wants to get into the act. Neither experience nor linguistic evidence is sufficient to dispel the so-called illusion of the self, but Steven Pinker suggests that neuroscience is able overcome the myth of the ghost in the machine: "Cognitive neuroscientists have not only exorcised the ghost but have shown that the brain does not even have a part that does exactly what the ghost is supposed to do: review all the facts and make a decision for the rest of the brain to carry out. Each of us *feels* that there is a single 'I' in control. But that is an illusion that the brain works hard to produce."[21] If there is no ghost and if the brain is the source of all intellectual functions, then there is absolutely nothing capable of reviewing all the facts and making a decision. One wonders, then, who it was who examined the evidence and decided on the conclusion asserted in this passage. There is no single Steven Pinker in control; no ghost either, and apparently not the brain. Presumably a unified conscious self was not responsible for this passage. Is this a message found in a bottle? Actually, this turns into an argument for the old ego; since the brain does not perform these intellectual functions, there must be something else to do the job.

I have no doubt, however, that someone, probably Steven Pinker, did review all the facts, because in the next paragraph he states: "One of the most dramatic demonstrations of the illusion of the unified self comes from the neuroscientists Michael Gazzaniga and Roger Sperry, who showed that when the surgeons cut the corpus callosum joining the cerebral hemispheres, they literally cut the self in two, and each hemisphere can exercise free will without the other's advice or consent."[22] However, the split-brain experiment proves nothing of the sort. What it does show is that the brain contains the physical machinery necessary for a unified self, and that when the machinery is disrupted, so is the unity of the self. Nothing in the thought experiment of Leibniz's mill requires us to doubt the dependence of various functions of the self upon the machinery of the body. Such dependence is also consistent with the fact that many changes in the body are dependent upon the unified self, as when a person decides to take a walk and thus causes his feet to move. This position is sometimes called *two-sided interaction,* and, it would appear, this is the view that ordinary human experience supports.

But Pinker rejects the verdict of ordinary human experience. "The conscious mind—the self or soul—is a spin doctor, not the commander in chief. . . . Often our conscious minds do not control how we act but merely tell us a story about our actions."[23] Of course, the story must be mistaken, because the chief character refers to itself as 'I' and takes responsibility for its actions. Pinker here approaches the view called *epiphenomenalism* or the *automaton theory,* according to which the brain does all the work and the mind passively mirrors some of the brain's activity.[24] It is like *Hamlet* without Hamlet. Epiphenomenalism is a form of one-sided interaction. It is implausible on its face because it denies any function to consciousness, an idea not only contrary to everyday experience but inconsistent with natural selection. Why should nature go to such trouble to produce consciousness if it does not serve any function, except as a repository of human vanity? In any case, Pinker does not quite arrive at epiphenomenalism, because for him the conscious self does have a function, namely, to tell false stories to itself and others. And since it tells them to others, it must be capable of getting the brain and tongue to act. So his effort to exorcise the ghost in the machine merely arrives at a somewhat attenuated version of two-sided interaction.

BEING IN THE WORLD

Human beings are passive in some respects and active in others. They are capable of being affected, for good or ill, by the impact of environmental forces. In particular, through their senses, they receive data capable of serving as information about their surroundings. Their capacity to act means that that they are in control to a certain extent of external intrusions and of the data they receive. As active agents, capable of learning, memory, thought, deliberation, foresight, choice, and action, persons qualify as substances retaining identity through time, from birth to death. The question of the unity of the stream of conscious experiences that Hume and James unsuccessfully attempted to answer must be enlarged to include the question of the identity of the person. The first-person point of view includes not merely the subjective events of consciousness but the acts of agents seeking what is good and avoiding evil. Persons are, as Heidegger, Dewey, and Wittgenstein emphasized, beings in and of the world, where 'world' includes material nature, as well as other selves and living beings. Persons have bodies as well as minds. Leibniz was correct in noting that a stroll through the brain omits an essential feature of the human person, namely, thought and perception, but it also omits the fact of being in the world, in which the body plays an indispensable role.

As Descartes emphasized, body and mind intermingle. Descartes stressed the fact of thinking as essential to the self, on the ground that one can doubt the existence of the body but not of thinking. However, this epistemic criterion of the human essence is one-sided. Some of the things that are doubted by Descartes in the First Meditation may turn out to be indispensable aspects of the self once the doubt has been overcome. Active agency or being-in-the-world becomes an essential category, once Descartes has noted that thinking includes the will and that the will is that aspect of the self that controls its worldly conduct. Acts of thought are themselves usually under the control of the will, so the will enters into the very nature of thinking.

Once Descartes has shown that we may trust our senses to some extent and under certain conditions and that we are entitled to accept the existence of our own bodies and the material world, then the fact that we are beings in and of the world is incorporated into the essential nature of the self. The self possesses a first-person point of view not only of its inner stream of consciousness but also of its worldly conduct. Those of its voluntary actions in which it goes beyond "mere" thinking in order to engage with things and persons within the world are under the control of the will. Its actions within the world are not mere motions of the body but bodily events whose fundamental descriptions are constituted by reference to the self's inner intentions and ends. The self in action is a unity of the 'I think' and the body, an intermingling, in Descartes' terms, of mind and body.

A common tendencey of thinkers who emphasize being-in-the-world as an essential structure of the self is to berate Descartes for, in Heidegger's words, "a vicious subjectivizing."[25] For example, Descartes' distinction between self and body is one of the philosophical dualisms that Dewey attempts to extirpate by leaning toward a behaviorist point of view. Wittgenstein has contributed a lengthy though obscure argument against the very idea of a private language.

Heidegger points out, correctly in my opinion, "that Descartes is 'dependent' upon medieval scholasticism and employs its terminology."[26] This is not, for Heidegger, an historical aside, but is intended as a criticism, as part of his "destructive retrospect of the history of ontology."[27] He refers with approval to Scheler's claim that "the person is no Thing-like and substantial being," and to the claim of Scheler and Husserl that "the unity of the person must have a Constitution essentially different from that required for the unity of Things of Nature. . . . Acts are something non-psychical. Essentially the person exists only in the performance of intentional acts, and is therefore essentially *not* an object."[28] By adopting the notion of substance that medieval scholasticism had taken over from Aristotle's metaphysics and by using it for his own purposes, however, Descartes had employed a category according to which the human person becomes merely one thing among others in nature. If Heidegger is correct in this indictment, then, under the assumption that science presupposes a materialistic ontology (an assumption I will later argue is mistaken), we can see that Descartes' conception of the self is easily transformed into a physicalistic one in which the 'I think' is reinterpreted as 'My brain thinks'.

According to Descartes, the human being is a compound substance composed of body and mind, and the mental component is what distinguishes it from other things in nature. Why then is Descartes' subjectivizing vicious? Heidegger suggests an answer in the following passage:

> When, however, we come to the question of man's Being, this is not something we can simply compute by adding together those kinds of Being which body, soul, and spirit respectively possess—kinds of Being whose nature has not as yet been determined. And even if we should attempt such an ontological procedure, some idea of the Being of the whole must be presupposed. But what stands in the way of the basic question of Dasein's Being (or leads it off the track) is an orientation thoroughly coloured by the anthropology of Christianity and the ancient world.[29]

This is a profound remark, but it is difficult to know how to respond to it, because it raises questions that are perhaps unanswerable. Merely adding body and mind together, Heidegger claims, fails to provide the distinctive unity and mode of being of the human person or *Dasein.* Of course, Descartes does not simply add them together but insists upon their intermingling, which consists, in the first place, of two-sided causal interaction and, in the second place, of the projection of consciousness throughout the body in the form of feeling. I have also emphasized a third, namely, the role of the will in guiding and controlling the motions of the body and, in this way, constituting human action and conduct. Heidegger insists that there are structures of the human person that fail to be incorporated into this picture, but it is not obvious that this is correct. A living animal or plant is a complex made up of organic parts interacting with one another to provide unity of behavior as well as adaptation to the environment. The concept of substance does not stand in the way of the unity in difference of living beings, so it is not clear how it stands in the way of the unity in difference of the human person. If Cartesian dualism is capable of explaining the mode of togetherness of body and mind, it is not clear what more needs to be done.

PERSONAL IDENTITY

The question of personal identity arises in two contexts at least. In the first place, we use different names, descriptions, or designations to refer to a person or persons, and we may wonder, in a particular case, whether the terms refer to the same or a different person. Thus, we know that 'George Washington' and 'the first president of the United States' designate one and the same person, whereas 'John Adams' and 'the third president of the United States' designate different ones. The question is not inherently a linguistic one. It concerns the characteristics mentioned in these designations and pertains to the question of whether the same or different persons exemplify them. In the second place, people change over time, and the changes can be quite radical in nature. Consider anyone at the time of his birth and that same person many years later. If the changes are radical enough, we may come to doubt our ascription of identity and wonder whether these are the same or different persons.

Questions such as these may arise for any substance. In fact, the concept of identity applies to anything and is not confined to substances. Questions of identity frequently have important practical consequences. For example, was the pistol found in John Smith's apartment the same as the one used in the killing of James Jones? Was John Smith the person who killed James Jones?

When you meet someone you know, you can tell who it is by his personal appearance, including physical characteristics, behavior, voice, and so forth. Some years ago, I happened to bump into someone I had last seen when we were children thirty years previously. Yet we recognized one another immediately. Although there had been vast changes in our appearance, there must have been some specific structural similarities that were the bases of the recognition. Something persisted throughout the changes, although it would not be easy to formulate in words what it was. The question whether John Smith murdered James Jones may come down to the identification of fingerprints on the murder weapon. This illustrates the fact that it is not just appearance that is used to identify persons, but even such specific characteristics as fingerprints, DNA, blood type, dental work, and so forth. The criminal justice system specializes in inventing and deploying methods of personal identification as part of its task of apprehending breakers of the law. Methods of identification making use of personal appearance and other physical characteristics provide ways of determining *identity from the outside.*

But there are also determinations of *identity from the inside,* where by 'inside' I mean the subjective first-person point of view. Thus a person can tell immediately his name and many other facts about himself without looking in a mirror or gaining a view of his physical appearance and characteristics. Such facts about himself are immediately referred to *himself* and thus involve exercises of self-consciousness. Even though each of us changes over time, we can rely upon our personal memories to determine what we have done in the past. Personal memory is a form of representational consciousness in which past events are referred to the individual remembering them as something he himself has brought about or experienced. Personal memory thus involves self-consciousness, or reference to oneself as oneself. Of course, we do not remember everything that happened; events can be forgotten, or have aspects that we do not know, or can occur prior to the development of the capacity for personal memory. We fill in the gaps using the reports of others, documents, photographs, and so forth. A person continuously creates and sustains a detailed unified picture of himself over time throughout the vast changes of a lifetime until the mental decay of old age undermines the capacity for personal memory and death destroys the self entirely or its connection to the body.

These ways of determining identity may occasionally fail. A person may have changed so radically that even those closest to him may not recognize him. Or we may encounter someone who looks exactly like John Smith but who is actually his identical twin. Or a person may misremember or forget something or lose his memory entirely as a result of disease or injury. I may no longer know who I am, and others may have no way of telling either. This suggests that the various ways of determining identity, although they are capable of supporting claims of identity and difference, are not logically conclusive grounds of identity. Perhaps personal identity consists of the sameness over time of a living human body. In general, the same material body is capable of sustaining its identity over vast changes through time. The table I write on looks completely different from the way it looked fifty years ago; one could not tell it is the same just by looking at it, even though it is the same. The aged John Smith lying in a hospital bed in a coma is the same person as the baby in this photograph. Can identity lie in anything but bodily continuity?

The main problem with this solution to the problem of identity is that in order for me to identify which of all the living human bodies is mine, I must relate it to myself and my subjective point of view. For example, *my* body is the one through whose eyes I see and, in general, the one whose sense organs provide me with experiences, a spatiotemporal location, and a perspective on the world. *My* body is the one in which I have feelings and which I use, in accordance with my decisions, to move about from place to place. That this body is mine is a contingent fact that could be imagined to be otherwise than it is. On the other hand, even if I should lose my memory, I could, in principle, retain an attenuated sense of self by thinking and being aware that I am thinking. So, it would seem, the self is prior to and distinct from its body; bodily marks of identity could one and all fail, while self-consciousness remains. This view is consistent with those accounts of identity that originate with Locke, according to which personal identity is constituted by consciousness or personal memory.[30] The self extends as far as consciousness extends; we fill in the gaps left by temporary cessations of consciousness, as in dreamless sleep, coma, anesthesia, and so forth, by the sorts of evidence already mentioned, but it is consciousness and nothing else that constitutes the basic framework and essential source of identity. In filling in these gaps, we of course must frequently make use of the body, but that is consistent with the Lockean position because the body cited has already been identified as the body of the self whose identity is in question.

Butler and Reid have decisively criticized the Lockean position.[31] According to their argument, when consciousness extends to the past in the form of personal memory, it discovers identity; it does not create it. For example, consider the fact that I now remember having done such and such at some time in the past. I can also imagine forgetting that I did it but being convinced that I did it by some document or human testimony. So, it would seem, it is a fact that I did it, and that fact can be retained in memory, or, if memory fails, it can be reached by means of other paths. There are different modes of access to the same fact, and this suggests that the fact is not constituted by any one of them but is simply there to be known. Moreover, personal memory presupposes the self and does not constitute it. Let us say that I remember having done X. My memory is not merely that X was done, from which I infer that it was done by me. After all, someone else could have done it, and, in that case, I might have found it difficult to determine who was responsible. Rather, I have a direct memory that I did it. Without the self already identified, there can be no personal memory at all; all memory of past events would be impersonal and leave open the question as to the identity of the responsible party.

Where does all this leave us? In reviewing the arguments, we considered various possibilities in which the usual marks of identity failed in some way or another. If we consider the failure of one mark at a time, whether from the outside or the inside, we could always rely upon other marks. Perhaps it is possible that almost all of them fail simultaneously, although, if the person continues to exist, an attenuated form of self-consciousness will remain.

Our determinations of identity are governed by a variety of marks belonging to the outside as well as to the inside. Those on the inside usually have priority, should there be a question raised when those on the outside fail—as when we ask identical twins which one is which. However, these marks seldom fail, and perhaps never in fact (as distinct from possibility) fail altogether. As they are always there to rely upon as long as life persists, we are seldom or never confronted with the logical puzzles that arise from imagined circumstances that deviate radically from those of everyday life. Once we have imagined possibilities that differ in important ways from the ways in which the world actually operates, we have cut loose from the marks that are the bases of our ordinary judgments of identity and we may not know what to say. In any case, our understanding of personal identity as revealed in the ways we resolve doubts in actual cases is consistent with the Cartesian picture, and the fact that the self is prior to the body in the ways indicated suggests that our sense of identity actually supports the Cartesian picture.

Chapter Four

PERCEPTUAL CONSCIOUSNESS

CONSCIOUSNESS

Earlier I characterized consciousness as a state of mind in which a person is aware of something. Understood in this way, consciousness is co-extensive with the mental, and it is what makes a state of a person a mental state. It takes various forms, among which are perceptual, sensory, representational, and introspective modes of being conscious. In this chapter, I shall discuss perceptual consciousness and its invariable attendant, sensory consciousness. I will begin by calling attention to some remarks of G. E. Moore about consciousness in his famous essay "The Refutation of Idealism."

Suppose I look at a red round chip and then at a chip exactly like the first, except that it is blue. Such experiences have a subject-object structure; each contains at least two constituents, the person or subject who is seeing something and the thing seen. In this case, I see not only the chips but their colors and other characteristics as well. Putting aside the subject or self for the moment, Moore claims that there are two other elements: "in every sensation or idea we must distinguish two elements, (1) the 'object,' or that in which one differs from the other; and (2) 'consciousness,' or that which all have in common—that which makes them sensations or mental facts."[1]

My seeing the red color of the first chip involves being conscious of its color; my seeing the blue color of the second involves also being conscious of its color. The experiences differ from one another in respect to the colors seen but are the same in respect to the consciousness, which is a constituent of both and is that which makes them mental facts.

But how does Moore know that when a person sees the blue color of an object there is this something that he calls consciousness? He recognizes that there is a difficulty here when he says:

> When we refer to introspection and try to discover what the sensation of blue is, it is very easy to suppose that we have before us only a single term. The term "blue" is easy enough to distinguish, but the other element which I have called "consciousness"—that which sensation of blue has in common with sensation of green—is extremely difficult to fix. That many people fail to distinguish at all is sufficiently shown by the fact that there are materialists. And, in general, what makes the sensation of blue a mental fact seems to escape us; it seems, if I may use a metaphor, to be transparent—we look through it and see nothing but the blue.[2]

A few pages later, Moore returns to this problem: "The moment we try to fix our attention upon consciousness and to see *what,* distinctly, it is, it seems to vanish: it seems as if it were diaphanous."[3] Because it is transparent or diaphanous, consciousness is introspectively indiscernible. And yet, in the very next sentence, Moore appears to contradict himself: "Yet it *can* be distinguished if we look attentively enough, and if we know that there is something to look for."[4]

So it turns out that consciousness *is* introspectively discernible because, although we do not discern it when "we try to fix our attention" upon it, we can discern it "if we look attentively enough" provided "we know that there is something to look for." But if we have not first spotted it through introspection, how can we know that there is something to look for?

Of course, this is very puzzling, and some philosophers have attempted to take another line entirely. For example, one explanation of why consciousness is transparent is that it is featureless. But if it is featureless, then it is a nonentity, and we can dispense with it entirely by adopting a behaviorist point of view.[5]

Moore's remarks on consciousness are incidental to the main purpose of his essay, which is to refute idealism. His refutation consists in claiming about "that peculiar relation which I have called 'awareness of anything'" that "this awareness is and must be in all cases of such a nature that its object, when we are aware of it, is precisely what it would be, if we were not aware."[6] That we are aware of anything makes no difference to the object. In fact, in *every* such case, the object exists independently of the fact that one is aware of it. Therefore, there is no reason to suppose, as idealism claims, that all facts are mental. Moreover, there is no intractable problem about our knowledge of an independent material world: "There is, therefore, no question of how we are to 'get outside the circle of our own ideas and sensations.' Merely to have a sensation is already to *be* outside that circle. It is to know something which is as truly and really *not* a part of *my* experience, as anything which I can ever know."[7]

In the Preface to *Philosophical Studies,* the book in which Moore reprinted "The Refutation of Idealism," he says of this essay that it "now appears to me to be very confused, as well as to embody a good many downright mistakes."[8] He does not tell us what the mistakes and confusions are, but it does not deserve to be repudiated in such a wholesale fashion. It raises, in a distinctive and original manner, the central question of the structure of consciousness and how it bears on our knowledge of the external world.

Moore thinks that a fact of consciousness is of the form 'X is aware of Y', where X is a person who is conscious, Y an object of which he is conscious, and awareness the relation that ties X to Y. He replies to idealism by claiming that Y is something that not only exists but that exists independently of X's being aware of it. Y belongs, therefore, to the external world and not to the circle of ideas. There are two immediate difficulties with this conception. In the first place, it neglects the existence of representational consciousness—the mere thought of something that may or may not be given to the senses and that may have no more claim to existence than Humpty Dumpty or Macbeth's dagger. Moreover, it is not self-evident, even with respect to sensory consciousness, that the thing of which one is aware exists. I shall discuss this later, but consider briefly the fact of visual afterimages. These are things of which we are directly conscious but for which there is no room either in matter or mind. One might conclude from afterimages that sensory awareness is not an infallible proof of existence, and that theoretical considerations might occasionally outweigh the direct evidence of the senses. But more of this later.

THE SENSES

We are accustomed to speak of the five senses, although other senses have been identified in the literature of psychology. What exactly do we have in mind when we speak of a sense? Connected to each sense is a sense organ, a part of the body whose functioning enables the sense to operate. A sense is a capacity of an animal, founded upon the activity of a sense organ, to become perceptually aware of various features of and changes in bodies and their environment. One sense is distinguished from the others by reference to the features that it enables us to discern perceptually. Certain features are unique to a sense, as colors are to the sense of sight or sounds are to hearing, whereas others are common to several senses, as shapes are detectible by both sight and touch. It is the unique features—or the proper sensibles, as they are called in the Aristotelian tradition—that demarcate one sense from another. Sight is that sense that enables us to see colors, hearing is the one that discerns sounds, smell informs us of odors, and so forth.

If we should come across an unfamiliar animal, we might wonder whether a certain physical organ is the basis of a sense and what sense it is. Is this organ in this fish the basis of hearing? If it is, then the fish uses it to become conscious of sounds. How do we determine this, since the fish is in no position to tell us anything directly? Experiments might provide a probable answer. Does the fish respond to sound waves directed at this organ? Is there any structure within the fish functionally analogous to the auditory structures of animals that we know possess the sense of hearing?

Suppose we are sure that a certain animal receives information by means of the activation of an organ on or near the surface of its body, but there is no analogy to any of the senses with which we are familiar. We may become convinced that it was using the organ to find its way in the world, just as a bat does in perceiving objects,[9] but we may be unsure of the nature of the perceptual experience that does the job. The question, What is it like to be a bat? has aroused interest in recent years. If we pursue the analogy with the human senses, we may wonder about the nature of the features that a bat's sense organs enable it to detect. What it is like to be a bat, then, comes down to what it is like to be a creature that is perceptually aware of a feature that perhaps we cannot become perceptually aware of because we lack a sense capable of discerning it. What could this feature be? What are we missing that the bat is aware of? Another instance of this problem pertains to the narwhale and its tusk. What function could a tusk have on a whale in arctic waters? Recently a group of scientists discovered that the tusk "forms a sensory organ of exceptional size and sensitivity"; they found that "10 million nerve endings tunnel from the tusk's core toward its outer surface, communicating with the outside world. . . . The nerves can detect subtle changes of temperature, pressure, particle gradients and probably much else, giving the animal unique insights."[10] What is it like to be a narwhale? Are the features that the tusk enables it to detect objects of a special form of consciousness, distinct from anything to be found in human perception?

There is something more to the question about the senses of the bat or the narwhale than the features they detect. Our sense organs are feature-detecting mechanisms that operate by making us *perceptually aware* of various features. That is, the information provided by the senses comes to us not just as information (as Descartes might say, as a pilot knows about the ship), but also as characteristics, events, relations, and objects manifested via perceptual awareness. Through sight, we acquire information about colors by seeing them; through taste, we find out about how objects taste by tasting them. In fact, we have reason to believe that our ability to perceive certain features is necessary to know their intrinsic nature, as distinguished from incidental facts about them. Thus, although a person blind from birth may know a lot about colors through studying the physiology of the human eye and the physics of light, he probably has no idea of what colors are in themselves. Although he would, in a sense, know a lot *about* colors, he would not know their intrinsic nature nor would he know what it is like to see a color. Since colors are in their nature objects of sight, without ever seeing them one would not know what they are. There is something unique in apprehending various things in the special and distinctive ways we become conscious of them in sense perception. These distinctive ways are *sense experiences*—special forms of awareness connected in regular ways to the physical operations of the sense organs and nervous system. If, indeed, humans do not know and perhaps are unable to know what it is like to be a bat, it is because the absence of a sense that a bat possesses makes it impossible to have certain experiences that a bat has. Nor, as

Leibniz's mill teaches us, would a study of the inner workings of the bat's nervous system put us in a position to imagine what it is like to be a bat, unless perhaps certain similarities between bat and human nervous systems let us infer some similarity between bat and human sense experience. That is what is meant by the privacy of experience.

FRAMEWORKS

In Plato's allegory of the cave, our commonsense understanding is represented by people who are constrained to observe flickering, shadowy images of objects projected upon the wall of a cave. They do not see the world as it really is but are aware only of images that fail to convey genuine knowledge of reality. In order to be able to grasp things as they really are, they must leave the cave or the world of everyday life, ascend from darkness into light, and attend not to ephemeral shadows but to real permanent things, illuminated by the light of the sun.

Plato's allegory suggests that there are two frameworks or conceptual schemes or systems of categories competing for our allegiance. The first is the framework of common sense, involving the categories we use in interpreting our experiences during the course of everyday practical life. This is the framework of the cave. The second is the instructed framework gained through philosophical reflection, in which we come to understand the limits and errors of the first framework and by which we are able to grasp things as they really are.

Some philosophers undertake to defend in various ways our commonsense understanding. For example, G. E. Moore describes his philosophical position in this way: "I am one of those philosophers who have held that the 'Common Sense view of the world' is, in certain fundamental features, *wholly* true."[11] This is a very guarded statement, for it leaves open the possibility that there are true propositions that do not belong to the truisms that Moore identifies with the commonsense view of the world. Moore does not deny that there are truths to be discovered outside the cave. On the other hand, since these commonsense truisms are wholly true and since he claims that we know them to be true, the commonsense view of the world is not something that would need to be revised, even if there are new truths to be learned by escaping from the cave.

P. F. Strawson distinguishes between two types of metaphysical inquiry. "Descriptive metaphysics is content to describe the actual structure of our thought about the world, revisionary metaphysics is concerned to produce a better structure."[12] The aim of descriptive metaphysics is "to lay bare the most general features of our conceptual structure." Common sense is not identified, as in Moore, with a set of truisms that are taken to be wholly true but with the conceptual framework that "lies submerged" beneath "the surface of language."[13] Strawson characterizes this submerged framework as a permanent, unchanging structure of thought:

> For there is a massive central core of human thinking which has no history—or none recorded in histories of thought; there are categories and concepts which, in their most fundamental character, change not at all. Obviously these are not the specialties of the most refined thinking. They are the commonplaces of the least refined thinking; and are yet the indispensable core of the conceptual equipment of the most sophisticated human beings.[14]

Although the framework of the cave constitutes "the commonplaces of the least refined thinking," it is, nevertheless, "indispensable." So revisionary metaphysics cannot replace it, and therefore one wonders whether there is any point to trying to produce "a better structure."

In any case, perceptual consciousness operates within the framework that descriptive metaphysics undertakes to describe. That framework underlies the ontological commitments that our perceptual judgments imply. Yet these commitments have not gone unchallenged in modern philosophy. What happens when the commonsense framework is examined in the light of "the specialties of the most refined thinking"? For example, Wilfrid Sellars remarks: "Although the framework of perceptible objects, the manifest framework of everyday life, is adequate for the everyday purposes of life, it is ultimately inadequate and should not be accepted as an account of what there is *all things considered.*"[15] After all, there is more to be considered than the commonplaces of the least refined thinking, and when that framework is put to the test by taking into account all the facts and theories brought to light in the process of inquiry, there is no reason a priori to suppose that it will remain unscathed. If there is an exit to the cave, we should leave it and enjoy the sunlight.

THE FRAMEWORK OF COMMON SENSE

By the framework of common sense I mean simply the world as it is revealed to perceptual consciousness in the course of the ordinary life of the ordinary person. In Hume's words, "It seems evident, that men are carried, by a natural instinct or prepossession, to repose faith in their senses; and that, without any reasoning, or even almost before the use of reason, we always suppose an external universe, which depends not on our perception, but would exist, though we and every sensible creature were absent or annihilated."[16] The faith in the senses of which Hume speaks is the belief that the things that one sees or hears or otherwise perceives exist independently of the perception of them. The table in front of me with its color and shape and the sounds produced as I tap on the keys of the keyboard would exist even if I had failed to perceive them. This is the presumption of the independent existence of the objects of sense perception.

I also think of this world as extending in space and time well beyond the particular scene that I now observe. I also think of my body as a thing within this world; the location of my body at this place and at this point in time creates the perspective or point of view that provides access to the scene I confront. Once I realize how extensive the world is and how minute in comparison is the scene before my eyes, I recognize that the senses afford, at best, a glimpse of a small portion of an independent world. As I move from place to place, I traverse a path within this world; the changing scenes multiply the glimpses I obtain, allowing me to synthesize them into a mental map of the wider world.

Some things within this wider world I learn about through inference, as when distant smoke tells me of a fire hidden behind a hill. However, I do not always need to infer the existence of the things that make up this scene that I now observe; perceptual consciousness tells me of many of them directly. Perceptual consciousness is not a form of representational consciousness. In it, things are given. What is given, the primordial data of the senses within the framework of common sense, can be identified by listing the things that I see, that I hear, that I taste, touch, and smell.

It is important to note that the terms used to identify and describe the items that are given are not necessarily immediately verifiable by reference to the data of perceptual consciousness. I pass a man on the street; his name is Harry Smith; he is, however, a stranger to me, and while his friends may identify him by sight, I cannot. I do not see him as Harry Smith; I do not know that it is Harry Smith that I see. A person just emerging for the first time from a tropical jungle may see the computer on which I am writing these words without recognizing that what he is seeing is a computer.

Thus, we must distinguish perceptual consciousness itself, in which things are given, from the concepts, names, and descriptions that apply to such things and that allow us to assert and deny propositions that can be either true or false. Perceptual consciousness does not assume the form of propositions capable of exemplifying a truth-value; truth and falsehood emerge when we use words and concepts to characterize and represent objects. Thus, seeing something should not be confused with seeing that it is such and such.[17] That something is seen, that it occupies my field of vision, is one thing; that it has this character, or is of that type, or bears that name, or stands in this relation to that is not the work of perceptual consciousness but the work of judgment, in which I draw upon my conceptual repertoire to apprehend the thing seen in the light of truth.

Some philosophers of perception have tried to distinguish between two forms of seeing. The first is *simple seeing,* in which both the native of the tropics and I see the computer. The second is *seeing that,* in which I see that it is a computer and he does not. However, this distinction is a mistake. We usually use the *seeing that* locution in contexts in which we wish to record something we have learned, such as when I see that a certain conclusion follows from certain premises. 'I see that' just means 'I realize that' or 'I now know that' or similar phrases. 'I see that' has no essential connection with visual consciousness, although we can use the phrase to record what we have learned from seeing something. What we learn depends both upon the concepts we have available and our background knowledge. Thus, I can truthfully claim to see that there is fire in the distance because I have learned of it by seeing the smoke and knowing that fire accompanies smoke. Instead of saying with Searle and McDowell that *all* seeing is seeing that, I want to claim instead that *no* seeing is seeing that. When I see that such and such is the case as a result of seeing something, I am thereby interpreting what I see by characterizing it as such and such. According to the framework of common sense, perceptual interpretations or judgments are not invariably the product of inferences in which one thing is a sign of something else, but they can be direct subsumptions of perceived items under concepts. The perceived items can be given directly, as when I see a certain color and then judge that it is red. In some cases, inferences are necessary in order to construct an interpretation. For example, when I label what I see as a computer, I am using my knowledge of features characteristic of computers to generate the interpretation 'That is a computer'. The constellation of seen characteristics that constitutes the mark of a computer becomes represented in premises from which I infer 'This is a computer'. How the mind is able to move from seeing the characteristics to conceptualizing them in such a way as to trigger the intended description is not something we know. But that we are able to interpret the world in this manner is known without question, for we perform such acts almost every moment of our waking lives.

SENSE AWARENESS

Human perceptual awareness was explained commonsensically by reference to the forms of awareness manifested in the exercise of the five senses. I have used the term 'perceptual consciousness' for this way of being aware of the world, and I have sharply distinguished it from such matters as seeing that, perceptual judgment, and inference, all of which essentially involve the use of items drawn from our conceptual repertoire to interpret what is given in sense experience. If one knows what it is like to see or hear or otherwise perceive something, then one knows what perceptual consciousness is.

Reflection upon the nature of sense experience soon makes us aware that another factor, sense awareness or sensory consciousness, is involved as a constituent of some, if not all, forms of perceptual consciousness. When

I run my finger over the surface of the desk I find that it is smooth, whereas running my finger over the surface of a piece of sandpaper tells me that it is rough. 'Smooth' and 'rough' designate textures of objects accessible through the sense of touch. I am able to become aware of the smoothness of the desk because it feels smooth, and this means that in running my finger over its surface, I feel a sensation in the finger that makes me aware of the desk and its texture. It would be a mistake to say that I infer the smoothness of the desk from the feeling in my finger; my perceptual awareness of the smoothness is not propositional in form and in itself does not involve the application of any concepts, although concepts immediately come into play as soon as I realize that that desk is smooth. Tactual feelings in one's finger and other parts of the body constitute a form of consciousness whose function is to make one aware of the texture, temperature, shape, and other features of bodies. In perceptual consciousness, we do not normally pay much attention to such feelings, because we are attending to the objective features of the bodies with which we come into contact. However, with effort, we are capable of attending to the feelings alone, and we then realize that perception by touch makes us aware of bodies and their features by means of sensations that exist only as we feel them. In Berkeley's terms, their *esse* is *percipi.* They are constituents not of the objective world that we apprehend but of the subjective stream of consciousness.

Psychology has entrenched in our thought a sharp distinction between the apprehension of an objective independent world through sense perception and the apprehension of items in the subjective stream of consciousness via introspection. If tactile sensations belong to the subjective stream, and if the feeling of them is indispensable in perception of the independent world through the sense of touch, then introspection is itself a component of sense perception. In perceptual awareness I feel the smoothness of the desk; in introspection, I am conscious of the accompanying feelings in my fingers, whether or not I am fully attending to them. Furthermore, it is necessary to distinguish the introspective awareness of the feelings from the interpretation that I make of them when I judge that I am experiencing feelings in my finger. In perceptual and introspective consciousness, items are given, and, in virtue of being given, they become available as topics for perceptual and introspective judgments.

Similar remarks apply to the senses of taste and smell. In these cases as well, the apprehension of features of objects—their tastes and odors—is mediated by introspectible bodily sensations located in the sense organ. Keep in mind that the concept of introspection illustrates the same duality as does the notion of perception. As cases of awareness, both are modes in which objects are given. But once something is given, it can be made a topic of judgment and interpretation, and in such cases the mode of consciousness is of representational form, in which concepts are applied to the things that are given.

TWO CONCEPTIONS OF THE GIVEN

Earlier in this chapter, I characterized perceptual consciousness as a form of awareness in which things and some of their characteristics are given. I also indicated that various bodily sensations implicated in certain forms of perceptual consciousness (namely, touch, taste, and smell) are given as well. These are cases of sensory consciousness. That something is given in general means that our awareness of it is non-inferential, non-conceptual, and non-representational. I adopt C. I. Lewis's suggestion that there are two further criteria of the given that apply to sensory and perceptual consciousness: "These are, first, its specific sensuous or feeling-character, and second, that the mode of thought can neither create nor alter it—that it remains unaffected by any change of mental attitude or interest."[18] In virtue of being given, various items are available as topics for judgment and interpretation.

In tasting the taste of a lemon, I find that both the sour taste of the lemon and the quality of the sensation that conveys that taste are given. We can say that the sensory quality is a sign of the taste of the lemon or contains information about its taste, as long as we recognize that it takes thought and judgment for sensory qualities to function as signs or to convey information. The sensation itself simply *makes* me aware of the taste of the lemon. The senses of taste, of smell, and of touch are ordered in such a way that bodily sensations function to cause perceptual awareness. In these cases, the relation between sensory and perceptual consciousness is that of cause to effect. The sensory qualities given in sensory consciousness are, according to Peirce's classification, indexical signs because their relation to what they signify is grounded in causation.[19]

But there is a distinction to be made in the ways in which they are given. If you ask the average person who knows nothing about the scientific understanding of how these three senses work about the nature of the heat that he apprehends when he touches a hot stove, or the nature of the sour taste of the lemon, or the nature of the foul smell given off by a skunk, his answer will be that he knows nothing of what they are as intrinsic features of the things perceived. For him, the heat of the stove is manifested in its capacity to produce these sensations; the taste of a lemon or the smell of a skunk is known only as the disposition of an object to produce these sensations in our sense organs. In these cases, perceptual awareness provides no information about the inner nature of the characteristics of which one is aware. But sensory awareness, that is, the introspective awareness of bodily sensations, does make us aware of its objects; the sensible qualities of these sensations are not merely unknown occult qualities whose effects are experienced, but they are manifest and revealed as what they are in experience. Of course, there is much more to know about them, especially their neural conditions, but that knowledge takes us beyond sensory consciousness into the framework of scientific understanding. To mark this distinction, I shall co-opt a term of Whitehead's and say that in sensory consciousness, the sensory qualities that are felt are given in the form of *presentational immediacy.*[20] Qualities that are given in this way I have earlier designated by the term *qualia.* Thus, in the operation of these three senses, we are made conscious of certain objective features of bodies as well as of certain qualia or qualitative features directly and immediately presented in sensory consciousness. These are two distinct ways in which something can be said to be given to the senses.

THE CORPUSCULARIAN HYPOTHESIS

Unlike the three senses discussed in the previous section, hearing and vision are not invariably or routinely accompanied by bodily sensations. In these senses there appears to be no duality between perceptual and sensory consciousness. However, the tendency in modern philosophy has been to insist that there is a sensory component in all forms of perceptual consciousness, not merely in those that incorporate bodily sensations. Take, for example, Locke: "For, since the things the mind contemplates are none of them, besides itself, present to the understanding, it is necessary that something else, as a sign or representation of the thing it considers should be present to it: and these are *ideas.*"[21] In his account of perceptual consciousness in general, Locke employs the term 'idea' to stand for the sensory component or quale that functions as an indexical sign of the objective quality that is given. Ideas are given in the form of presentational immediacy, and it is by means of ideas that the features of bodies, both primary and secondary, are also given. Following Locke, I shall distinguish between things given immediately—the items of presentation immediacy—and those given indirectly as a result of the operation of the former.

The sensory manifold composed of the qualia of presentational immediacy and their interrelations constitutes the ways in which bodies and their environments appear to us. Perceptual consciousness is constituted by the ways in which they appear. Locke provides us with a *causal theory* of the origin of appearances:

> If then external objects be not united to our minds when they produce *ideas* in it and yet we perceive *these original qualities* in such of them as singly fall under our senses, it is evident that some motion must be thence continued by our nerves or animal spirits, by some parts of our bodies, to the brains or the seat of sensation, there to *produce in our minds the particular* ideas *we have of them.* And since the extension, figure, number, and motion of bodies of an observable bigness may be perceived at a distance *by* the sight, it is evident some singly imperceptible bodies must come from them to the eyes, and thereby convey to the brain some *motion,* which produces these *ideas* which we have of them in us.[22]

These motions that Locke refers to are the motions of the "insensible parts"[23] of bodies. Here he brings into play his acceptance of "the corpuscularian hypothesis, as that which is thought to go furthest in an intelligible explication of the qualities of bodies."[24]

By "the corpuscularian hypothesis," Locke is referring to the revival of the ancient atomism of Democritus in the natural philosophy of his time, according to which the bodies we perceive are composed of "insensible parts" or "imperceptible bodies." Material nature consists of nothing but atoms and clumps of atoms moving in space through periods of time. The atoms themselves have primary qualities "such as are utterly inseparable from the body," such as solidity, extension, shape, and motion. In addition, bodies exemplify secondary qualities, which "are nothing in the objects themselves but powers to produce various sensations in us by their *primary qualities,* i.e. by the bulk, figure, texture, and motion of their insensible parts, as colours, sounds, tastes, etc."[25]

Since Locke's time, physics has developed a much more complex account of the nature of bodies than Locke could have conceived. The "insensible parts" of nature combine, in ways that are barely intelligible to us, features of particles and of waves. We can still make use of the notion of a primary quality, but we must interpret it as an evolving concept that specifies the irreducible characteristics of the fundamental constituents of matter as well as of the bundles of these constituents that we perceive as bodies as specified by the physics or natural philosophy of the time. Common sense, uninstructed by science, knows nothing of the existence and intrinsic nature of the fundamental constituents, so it is constrained to conceive many of the perceived features of bodies merely as powers or potentialities or dispositions of bodies to appear in certain ways.

Sounds and colors, objectively conceived, are not, for Locke, occurrent properties of matter, as they seem to uninstructed common sense; they are merely potentialities of bodies to appear in certain ways. The qualia that these potentialities produce in the mind are among the subjective forms that constitute the ways that bodies appear, as distinct from the objective features revealed in natural philosophy. The awareness of occurrent colors and sounds, therefore, is an instance of sensory rather than perceptual consciousness. We say we see colors and hear sounds, and this way of speaking may certainly be retained. But the seeing and the hearing that have occurrent qualia as their objects are forms of introspective consciousness directed at items of presentational immediacy, rather than forms of perceptual consciousness that provides a glimpse of the objective world.

COLOR AND CONSCIOUSNESS

Max Weber frequently cited Friedrich Schiller's phrase 'the disenchantment of the world' to designate a salient characteristic of the modern worldview. Scientific inquiry with its foundation in empirical knowledge "has consistently worked through to the disenchantment of the world and its transformation into a causal mechanism."[26] Descartes' mind/body dualism and Locke's appropriation of the corpuscularian hypothesis and the Newtonian conception of law as the basis for his ontology of nature mark a crucial stage in the disenchantment of the world: magic and miracles are discredited, the gods retreat to their own abode, and the qualitative features of matter are subjectivized. Here is how Whitehead characterizes the outcome of this intellectual transformation:

> Thus nature gets credit which in truth should be reserved for ourselves: the rose for its scent; the nightingale for his song; and the sun for his radiance. The poets are entirely mistaken. They should address their lyrics to themselves, and should turn them into odes of self-congratulation on the excellency of the human mind. Nature is a dull affair, soundless, scentless, colourless: merely the hurrying material, endlessly, meaninglessly.[27]

How did the poets come to be mistaken? How does one get from the claim that visible bodies are bundles of atoms to the conclusion that they are colorless?

Here is Locke's argument in brief: "Why are whiteness and coldness in snow, and pain not, when it produces the one and the other *idea* in us; and can do neither, but by the bulk, figure, number, and motion of its solid parts?"[28] Just as the primary qualities of objects cause us to feel pain on impact upon the sense organ of touch, so these same primary qualities cause the snow to look white as they impinge upon the apparatus of the sense of sight. Just as we ascribe pain to ourselves and not to the object, so we should ascribe color to ourselves and not to the object. That is why the poets are mistaken.

But, one might ask, why can't the snow both appear and be white? Why should the scientific story lead to the subjectivization of the secondary qualities and not of the primary qualities? To answer this, it is necessary to identify an unstated premise in Locke's argument. We do not ascribe pain to the object because that would be unnecessary in order to explain why we feel pain when we come into contact with it. We are making use here of a version of Ockham's razor, according to which the objective features of bodies are those necessary to explain (in accordance with the current natural philosophy) why bodies appear the way they do. That something is square may be necessary to explain why it looks square; that something is actually moving may be necessary to explain why it appears to move. Thus the primary qualities enjoy objective existence. But that the snow is actually white is not necessary to explain why it looks white; all that is necessary is that the snow consists of a clump of invisible particles that act upon the eyes in a certain way. Thus, the poets violate Ockham's requirement of simplicity by unnecessarily duplicating the qualitative features of experience.

The poets agree with common sense in accepting the resemblance hypothesis, according to which the qualities that matter appears to exemplify, it really does exemplify. Locke, however, modifies the resemblance hypothesis in this way: "the *ideas of primary qualities* of bodies *are resemblances* of them, and their patterns do really exist in the bodies themselves; but the *ideas produced* in us *by* these *secondary qualities have no resemblance* of them at all. There is nothing like our *ideas* existing in the bodies themselves."[29] Just as the smell of the rose is nothing like the sensation that the rose produces, just as the taste of the lemon is nothing like the sensation the lemon produces, so the appearance of color is nothing like the configuration and motions of the atoms that cause appearances of color. Color, sound, and all the other secondary qualities exist not in the material world but in consciousness. They are phenomena of sensory consciousness, items in the manifold of sense, not properties of bodies.

CORPUSCLES AND COMMON SENSE

Locke claims that there are two distinct uses for our terms for secondary qualities. In one use they designate immediately given ideas of sensation, such as the color I see when I see a lemon. In the other use, they represent qualities of bodies "which are nothing in the objects themselves but powers to produce various sensations in us." The yellow color that is indirectly given to me is really the capacity or power of the lemon to cause me to have this experience in virtue of its atomic structure; the color that I see is really an introspectible quality of a sensory item that belongs to my stream of consciousness.

Our ordinary use of a term like 'yellow', however, incorporates no such duality in its meaning. When I report both that the lemon looks yellow and that it is really yellow, I am claiming that the color that it looks to have is the same as the color it really does have. Our commonsense understanding does not allow that there are two sorts of colors, those given in sensation and those given as objective features of objects; all colors are objective features of matter that may or may not appear as they really are. This is the framework of common sense that, according to Hume, leads men "to repose faith in their senses . . . we always suppose an external universe, which depends not on our perception, but would exist, though we and every sensible creature were absent or annihilated." Colors belong to this "external universe"; sensory appearances are the ways in which colors are given.

Locke's argument leads to a point of view inconsistent with the framework of common sense. Wilfrid Sellars entitles that framework, cherished by the poets, the *manifest image;* in the light of the considerations brought forward by Locke, Descartes, and others, Sellars proposes that it should be replaced in our philosophical thinking by the disenchanted *scientific image* or framework.[30] Locke wishes to remain within the framework of common sense; that is why he retains a use for color names in which they designate objective properties of matter. It would be too much of a shock to say outright that lemons are not really yellow or that tomatoes are not really red. Yes, they are really yellow and really red in the sense that they really possess these powers.

Earlier I claimed with respect to the objective qualities given by the senses of touch, taste, and smell that what ordinary thought knows of them are the powers or potentialities of objects to cause certain sensations. Science tells us what they really are, but in ordinary life we know only that they produce these sensations. But even within the framework of common sense, they are not, as Locke claimed, *mere* powers; they are unknown occurrent features of objects that constitute the basis of known powers to produce certain sensations. We think, for example, that the heat of the stove really is something in the stove, but we know nothing about it except that it is able to cause sensations of heat when we touch it. Heat is indirectly given as something capable of generating such sensations.

The case is different with regard to colors and sounds. We think that experience is sufficient to inform us about their nature; we also think of them as occurrent objective features. What Locke's argument shows is that they are not objective features at all, but qualia embedded in fleeting sensory events within the stream of consciousness. The manifest image is correct in the thought that colors and sounds are immediately given occurrent qualities, but incorrect in thinking of them as objective. The scientific image informs us of their causes and neural accompaniments and conditions; it tells how creatures endowed with the sense of sight become aware of the world through these modalities of experience. But it disenchants the world by subjectivizing these qualities, and thus annoys the poets. Locke recognizes that common sense does not get things completely right when he says that secondary qualities are "commonly thought to be the same in those Bodies, that those *Ideas* are in us."[31] What Locke should have said, when he recognized that what is commonly thought is mistaken, is that lemons are not really yellow and tomatoes not really red even though we are constrained, via the tendency noted by Locke and Hume and exploited by the poets, to project psychic additions upon the world.

THE GREAT DECEPTION OF SENSE

In his *Elements of Law,* Thomas Hobbes makes this sweeping claim: "Whatsoever accidents or qualities our senses make us think there be in the world, they are not there, but are seemings and apparitions only. The things that really are in the world without us, are those motions by which the seemings are caused. And this is the great deception of sense."[32] Hobbes adopts a more radical view than does Locke. For Locke, the resemblance hypothesis correctly applies to the primary qualities but is mistaken for the secondary. Hobbes, on the contrary, claims that all appearances are deceptive: "The things that really are in the world without us" are merely particles in motion. The edge of my desk, for example, appears perfectly straight and at rest, but should we be able to apprehend its atomic structure, it would appear quite irregular and composed of moving particles. The manifold of sense in its entirety is something subjective, mere "seemings and apparitions."

To those whose views of matter are uninstructed by the corpuscularian hypothesis, and even to those who are instructed but presently occupied with practical concerns, the things of which we are directly aware seem be "in the world without us." This is the great deception of sense: "And though at some certain distance, the reall and very object seem invested with the fancy it begets in us; Yet still the object is one thing, the image or fancy is another. So that Sense in all cases, is nothing els but originall fancy, caused (as I have said) by the pressure, and is by the motion, of externall things upon our Eyes, Eares, and other organs thereunto ordained."[33] The seemings that are within us are *projected* upon the external world so that "the reall and very object seem invested with the fancy it begets in us." These seemings or images strike us as being things in the external world, although they are merely mental additions produced by the impacts of the particles upon our sense organs.

One way of interpreting Hobbes' account of the great deception of sense is to recognize that the sensory manifold presents us with, in Whitehead's terms, "simplified editions"[34] of complex and mostly unknown (except in a general way to the instructed) material processes that make up the natural world. Because of this "projective reference beyond the body,"[35] we fall into the error of taking what is really abstract and simplified for the concrete processes of nature. This Whitehead calls the "Fallacy of Misplaced Concreteness."[36] Although these abstractions give rise to false judgments because we mistakenly take them for the concrete realities themselves, they are, nevertheless, quite useful. If, in daily life, we were possessed of a perceptual mechanism that allowed us to apprehend nature as it really is in itself, independently of the normal operations of the senses, we would be unable to engage in practical action; we would find ourselves amidst a swirl of particles and waves, oblivious to things affecting us for good or ill. We can speculate that the simplified editions we employ to find our way about and the projective references that make them appear objective are products of natural selection that have survival value.

ARE WE REALLY DECEIVED?

Some philosophers who accept the Hobbesian point of view, that is, who endorse the idea that material things consist of nothing but particles in motion (as this would be understood in the light of modern physics), would still be reluctant to jettison our commonsense view that holds, for example, that lemons are yellow. Here is how Sellars understands the matter:

> Many years ago it used to be confidently said that science has shown, for example, that physical objects are not really coloured. Later it was pointed out that if this is interpreted as the claim that the sentence 'Physical objects have colours' expresses an empirical proposition which, though widely believed by common sense, has been shown by science to be false, then, of course, this claim is absurd. The idea that physical objects are not coloured can make sense only as the (misleading) expression of one aspect of a philosophical critique of the very framework of physical objects located in Space and enduring through Time. In short, 'Physical objects are not really coloured' makes sense only as a clumsy expression of the idea that there are no such things as the coloured physical objects of the common sense world, where this is interpreted, not as an empirical proposition—like 'There are no nonhuman featherless bipeds'—*within* the common sense frame, but as the expression of a rejection (in *some* sense) of this very framework itself, in favor of another built around different, if not unrelated, categories.[37]

Sellars' view implies that the claim that lemons are not really yellow, if interpreted as an empirical proposition verified by science, is "absurd" and "misleading."

On the other hand, Sellars also claims:

> And of course, as long as the existing framework is used, it will be *incorrect* to say—otherwise than to make a philosophical point *about the framework*—that no object is really coloured, or is located in Space, or endures through Time. But, *speaking as a philosopher,* I am quite prepared to say that the common sense world of physical objects in Space and Time is unreal—that is, that there are no such things. Or, to put it less paradoxically, that in

> the dimension of describing and explaining the world, science is the measure of all things, of what is that it is, and of what is not that it is not.[38]

I understand Sellars' view as the claim that the making of an empirical statement is implicitly accompanied with a reference to the framework within which it is being made. Within the framework of the manifest image or common sense, 'Lemons are yellow' is true. However, the scientific image as it is understood philosophically presupposes or implies that there are no colored objects. Assertions need to be interpreted relative to the frameworks in which they are made.

Sellars' discussion of the relation between science and common sense does not convince me of his interpretation of 'Lemons are yellow'. First, the sharp distinction between the commonsense and scientific frameworks is not something that exists within science and common sense as actually practiced. Our statements are normally not accompanied with a tag indicating the framework to which they belong. The contrast between the manifest and scientific images is a philosophically motivated distinction imposed upon a miscellaneous collection of statements, beliefs, opinions, and theories for the purposes of philosophical clarification. There is nothing wrong with the distinction as such, but because it is external to the actual use of language, it cannot be directly used to settle the semantic status of statements about color, whether made in science or common sense. Therefore, the distinction should not be used to determine the truth-value of 'Lemons are yellow', whether made by a person shopping for lemons or made by a physicist developing a theory of the causes of color.

Second, Sellars admits that science provides the materials and data on which the philosophical critique of the manifest image is based. If science is the measure of all things, then the correct way to determine the truth-value of 'Lemons are yellow' is to interpret the evidence of the senses in the light of the further evidence provided by the various sciences that study color. Under such an interpretation, the totality of the evidence shows that colors as seen are not objective features of bodies, but belong to the sensory order; they are denizens of sensory manifolds, not properties of material things. In short, lemons are not really yellow.

Of course, when, as philosophers, we attempt to tidy up the products of our overlapping language games by assigning statements to different frameworks, we will note that, when shopping for lemons, it is better to think that lemons are yellow than that they are blue or red. That is because the biological function of the sensory order is to produce indexical signs of objective features that have practical value. Operating within a practical context, we find that it is more useful to think that lemons are yellow because that is how most of our fellow humans see them. Because our everyday practical lives are dominated by practical considerations, in which we take the evidence of the senses as sufficient to fix belief, it does not occur to us to doubt that lemons are yellow. But when we return to our studies or our laboratories and examine the question in the light of the requirement of total evidence (as well as in the light of epistemic principles such as Ockham's razor), we are, I claim, forced to acknowledge that 'Lemons are yellow' is false. That is why, when we speak within the scientific image, we find it reasonable to assert that there are no colored material things. But we would not be forced to say, as philosophers, that there are no colored material things, if it were not for the fact that the totality of the empirical evidence requires us to admit that lemons, although they look yellow to almost everyone, are not really yellow. Yes, Hobbes was correct about "the great deception of sense."

SCIENTISM

Sellars claims that "science is the measure of all things, of what is that it is, of what is not that it is not." I shall adopt the term *scientism* for this view, where the term 'science' is used to designate what are today classified as the empirical sciences. There are philosophers who have argued for the thesis of the unity of the sciences. Some of them have offered an epistemic interpretation of this unity by reference to a unity of method. If that interpretation means that, at the most abstract level, there are procedures common to all the empirical sciences, such as perception, induction, hypothesis testing, and so forth, then the thesis of the epistemic unity of the sciences is true but banal. When one moves to a more concrete level, striking methodological differences emerge; the specific modes of inquiry, the instruments, the problematic situations, and the interest in laws of nature of physicists, psychologists, economists, historians, and anthropologists do not have much in common. The more interesting thesis of the unity of science is the metaphysical one according to which the various subject matters of all the sciences are reducible to one type. For example, Hobbes' view that reality consists of particles in motion and nothing but particles in motion, an early version of today's physicalism, is a materialist interpretation of metaphysical unity. I doubt that this version is true, and my discussion of Leibniz's mill and Descartes' dualism was intended to drive that point home. Since physicalism is the only form of unity currently on the table, I conclude, provisionally of course, that the metaphysical thesis of the unity of the sciences is mistaken.

For this reason, instead of speaking of science with a capital 'S', as if there was just one thing going on, I take 'science' to designate a plurality of different inquiries, sometimes overlapping, sometimes going their own way. What justifies calling them all by the term 'science' is that each of them has evolved in the past four hundred years or so into an organized community whose inquiries have a systematic empirical character. Most important of all, they aim to be objective, that is, to grasp their portion of reality as it is in itself, to gain the unvarnished truth about the ways the world works. They adopt reliable methods and procedures suitable for this purpose and aim at provisional agreements founded upon the use of such procedures. Because they are organized as communities of interacting investigators following reliable methods, they are able to cancel out one another's prejudices and personal inclinations; in this way they entertain the hope that their investigations will reveal what is false and create a path to what is true.

I take it that scientism as I have defined it is, at best, an exaggerated claim. After all, the diffuse and unorganized methods of inquiry of common sense are frequently able to gain the truth, and the methods used are often reliable. If I am looking for my wallet, I have ways and means of determining where it is. I too am able to gain a glimpse of the portion of reality that I inhabit. So science is not the exclusive measure of what is and of what is not. Moreover, I have limited science to empirical inquiry, and that leaves mathematics out of the picture. If one thinks of science not as *the* measure of what is but as *a* measure of what is, then it is controversial whether mathematics is a science. Whether pure mathematics has its own portion of reality to investigate, or whether it merely constructs abstract formal systems that have no metaphysical import but may turn out to be of use in the empirical and applied sciences, are questions still under discussion; the philosophy of mathematics has not achieved a lasting consensus and is unlikely to do so. However, mathematical inquiry in our time is conducted by an organized community whose members try to solve certain problems and employ various procedures in common, such as the method of proof, and who aim at definitive and certain truths about proposed solutions. Although mathematics is not an empirical science but, instead, employs a priori methods in its search for truth, because it is conducted by a community of inquirers and employs reliable criteria, it has certain similarities to the empirical sciences and is often considered to be a science in its own right.

I shall use the broader term *inquiry* to designate any systematic search for truth, whether in science, mathematics, philosophy, or everyday life. Philosophy too is a form of inquiry, but it is organized not into a single community of inquirers but into a number of smaller communities that tend to disagree with one another on fundamental issues. Philosophers tend to go off on their own and aim at consensus within their own subcommunity.

I said earlier that scientism is at best an exaggeration, but some have claimed that it is badly mistaken and that there are roads to truth other than the modes of inquiry that have been mentioned. This is an important topic for discussion, but, in its general form, it is not germane to the present investigation. However, in my discussion of color and the secondary qualities in general, I have relied upon scientific and philosophical considerations to support my contention that material things are not really colored. I will now turn to consider Whitehead's appeal to poetry to overturn this view.

POETS AND PHILOSOPHERS

Scientism is a philosophical, not a scientific claim. One can consistently be a scientist while at the same time thinking that there are other paths to knowledge. According to Whitehead, philosophy has a cognitive task distinct from the sciences:

> I hold that philosophy is the critic of abstractions. Its function is the double one, first of harmonising them by assigning to them their right relative status as abstractions, and secondly of completing them by direct comparison with more concrete intuitions of the universe, and thereby promoting the formation of more complete schemes of thought. It is in this respect that the testimony of the great poets is of such importance. Their survival is evidence that they express deep intuitions of mankind penetrating into what is universal in concrete fact. Philosophy is not one among the sciences with its own little scheme of abstractions which it works away at perfecting and improving. It is the survey of the sciences, with the special objects of harmony, and their completion. It brings to this task, not only the evidence of the separate sciences, but also its own appeal to concrete experience. It confronts the sciences with concrete fact.[39]

According to Whitehead, the empirical sciences construct a representation of the world that may very well be correct as far as it goes. But that represented world is an abstraction, a selection of material that is amenable to scientific treatment. Speaking of Wordsworth, Whitehead says, "he alleges against science its absorption in abstractions. His consistent theme is that the important facts of nature elude the scientific method."[40]

In particular, Whitehead objects to the subjectivizing of the secondary qualities:

> One reason [for distrusting subjectivism] arises from the direct interrogation of our perceptive experience. It appears from this interrogation that we are *within* a world of colours, sounds, and other sense-objects, related in space and time to enduring objects such as stones, trees, and human bodies. . . . But the subjectivist . . . makes this world, as thus described, depend on us, in a way which directly traverses our naïve experience. I hold that the ultimate appeal is to naïve experience and that is why I lay such stress on the evidence of poetry.[41]

Whitehead is correct in pointing out that from the standpoint of naïve experience, we dwell within a world of objects displaying secondary as well as primary qualities, not the Hobbesian world of minute particles in motion. That is how things appear, to us as well as to the poets. We think that the visual and auditory qualities that appear are not qualia embedded in a subjective sensible manifold but rather objective features of material objects. In Heidegger's terms (see chapter 3), we are beings in the world, not Cartesian selves directly aware only of their own sensory contents. From that standpoint, the Hobbesian world is an abstraction that leaves out what the poets cherish. Whitehead and Heidegger take their stands on the evidence of the senses. What shall we make of this?

THE EVIDENCE OF THE SENSES

Whitehead offers the following argument against the subjectivizing to which the poets also object: "I do not understand how a common world of thought can be established in the absence of a common world of sense. . . . It is difficult to see how the subjectivist is to divest himself of his solitariness."[42] Whitehead's ultimate appeal is not only to naïve experience but also to the familiar point that the subjectivist is defeated by an inability to refute solipsism. If one's sense experience yields direct information only about one's own subjective states, there is no basis for establishing the existence of a common objective world, much less a world of invisible particles in motion.

The starting point for Locke's argument about secondary qualities is an objective material world in which secondary qualities appear to be as objective as the bodies they appear to qualify. In answer to the question of the composition of the bodies that are perceived, Locke rejects the theory of hylomorphism characteristic of the Aristotelian tradition and adopts the newly revived corpuscularian hypothesis. His preference for the latter is based on the claim that it provides a better explanation for numerous phenomena, including human sense experience. The corpuscularian hypothesis is founded not directly upon naïve experience but upon abductive inferences that establish that it is a better explanatory theory than its competitors.

Of course, naïve experience provides the initial evidence in favor of the corpuscularian hypothesis. For example, the rain deposits a puddle of water on the sidewalk; the clouds dissipate; the sun shines upon the water; and after a while the puddle disappears. The corpuscularian hypothesis is able to explain the familiar facts of evaporation by supposing that the sun increases the temperature of the water in the puddle, that the increase in temperature causes the molecules of water to increase their acceleration, and that the increase of acceleration gradually causes the molecules to exit the puddle until no more remain. This abductive hypothesis explains the naïve experience of evaporation by a theory about the nature of water and of heat, according to which one would expect the puddle to dissipate. Hylomorphism, however, contributes nothing so plausible to explain evaporation.

Once the corpuscularian hypothesis is established by reference to such familiar facts, it can then be used to understand the facts of perceptual experience. One consequence of the explanation it provides is, as we have seen, the subjectivizing of secondary qualities. It becomes necessary to reinterpret the meaning of our experience: instead of thinking of the yellow color we see when we look at a lemon as a quality of the lemon, it is reinterpreted as a quale embedded in the sensory manifold. The scientific study of human experience leads us away from our naïve understanding of the nature and meaning of experience. As Hermann Weyl points out,

> The more modern science, especially physics and mathematics, strives to recognize nature as it is in itself or as it comes from God, the more it has to depart from the human, all too human ideas with which we respond to our practical surroundings in the natural attitude of our existence of strife and action. . . . For the philosophical and metaphysical import of science has not declined but rather grown through its estrangement from the naïve world of human conceptions.[43]

The naïve conception of experience is thus shown to be mistaken. The evidence of the senses is not rejected but reinterpreted.[44] What were taken according to the naïve conception as objective features of bodies are now understood as subjective indexical signs (ideas in Locke's terms) of objective features of imperceptible particles in motion and the clumps of particles that constitute the reality of the bodies we perceive. There is no threat of solipsism because, in the first place, the subjectivist position could not have been attained without the starting point of an objective world; second, the subjectivist position does not undermine the Hobbesian conception of matter, nor is it incompatible with it; and third, reliable procedures are in place that enable us to acquire knowledge of matter on the basis of subjective sense experience. Even though the ultimate appeal in our inquiries into the nature of matter is to sense experience, it is not to our naïve interpretation of experience but to an interpretation instructed by scientific inquiry.

What shall we say to the poets? We can tell them that they can still write about the colors of the flowers and the songs of the birds but that they should now understand that they are affected as we all are by the great deception of sense. Perhaps this understanding will influence their aesthetics. Art does not stand still any more than does science and philosophy.

THE MYTH OF THE GIVEN

Earlier in this chapter, I distinguished two ways in which something is given. In the first way, the given is just the perceived; anything that is an object of the senses is to that extent given: it is a datum of sense. The second way was introduced in considering the senses of touch, taste, and smell; perception via these senses involves bodily sensations that belong to the stream of consciousness. Bodily sensations are, then, immediately or directly given, whereas the perceived objects of these three senses are only indirectly given by means of the sensations. Further considerations established that colors and sounds and, in fact, the entire sensory manifold are among the items directly given, and these belong to the stream of consciousness as well. The qualitative features of the world are imported into the mental sphere, and what remains of matter is best understood in updated Hobbesian terms.

Wilfrid Sellars has criticized the concept of the given in his essay "Empiricism and the Philosophy of Mind" as a myth. The version of the alleged myth that I will now discuss does not dismiss the two concepts of the given I have just explained. Rather, it adds to the idea of the directly given the epistemic claim that the consciousness of sensory manifolds forms *the* foundation of empirical knowledge. This means that all knowledge of the physical and mental worlds is based upon premises reporting occurrences of items in subjective sensory manifolds. Knowledge begins with a direct consciousness of qualia embedded in sensory manifolds; the self then represents to itself or others what it apprehends and constructs its conception of the objective world through inference from what is directly given. In short, we start with sensory appearances, infer the objects and events of everyday life that we perceive through the senses on the basis of premises about how things appear, and then, by abductive and inductive inference, establish empirical generalizations and grand theories about the universe.

The basic argument for this version of the foundations of knowledge is that, in order to gain knowledge of the objective material world, one must have access to information about the world; sense perception is the only mode of access available to us in the world; and sense perception works by presenting the self with the ways things appear, what I have called sensory manifolds.

There are a number of good reasons for dismissing this model of human knowledge as a myth. First, naïve experience does not support this model; it presents itself as a direct access to the material world without the intervention, in the case of sight and hearing, of sensory consciousness in the form of visual and auditory manifolds. That colors and sounds are items within the subjective order of experience and not the material order of nature is a result of an argument that brings into play the existence of the material world and our scientifically instructed understanding of how sense experience is caused by the impact of physical events upon our sense organs. Thus, belief in an objective order of nature, rather than being the conclusion of an argument based on premises about the subjective order, is itself the starting point by which the existence of the subjective order is substantiated and its nature clarified. That colors and sounds are directly given items of the subjective manifold of sense is not the starting point and basis of knowledge, but is, rather, a conclusion of an argument whose premises are drawn from those established sciences concerned to understand the nature of color and sound. The point may be summarized in a somewhat paradoxical way by stating that the directly given is not given; it must be established by argument.

In the second place, the idea that our perceptual-based knowledge of the external world is derived from inferences whose premises report appearances is mistaken. Sense perception is not, as I have pointed out, a conceptual affair, in which denizens of the external world are represented to us. To see something is not to see that something is such and such, although once we have seen something we are usually in a position to form a perceptual judgment about it. Seeing an object consists merely in that object's appearing to us or looking to us in some way. In general, sense perception of objects consists of the ways that objects appear to us via the senses. Science then instructs us that the ways things appear are caused by the particular energies that strike the senses and that the connections between such causes and such effects are expressible in psychophysical laws.

Sensory appearances, then, are not products of conceptual activity or thought; they lack intentionality and intrinsic representational content, although they acquire a representational and informational function when used by the self as indexical signs to discover useful facts about its surroundings. This fact about them is sometimes missed because of the semantic ambivalence of the term 'appear' in ordinary talk. Sometimes we use 'appear' in perceptual judgments that express what we are inclined to believe, as when someone says of some animal that it appears to be a wolf. But sometimes we use 'appear' and related concepts to report not inclinations to believe but sensory items themselves, as when we say that although we know that lemons are yellow and we have no inclination to believe anything to the contrary, this lemon in this light looks orange.

A common thought among philosophers of perception who accept that there is such a thing as sensory consciousness—a directly given element in perception—is that the given is always accompanied by interpretation. Here, for example, is C. I. Lewis's point of departure:

> The given element is never, presumably, to be discovered in isolation. If the content of perception is first given and then, in a later moment, interpreted, we have no consciousness of such a first state of intuition unqualified by thought, though we *do* observe *alteration* and *extension* of interpretation of a given content as a psychological temporal process. A state of intuition unqualified by thought is a figment of the metaphysical imagination, satisfactory only to those who are willing to substitute a dubious hypothesis for the analysis of knowledge as we find it. The given is admittedly an excised element or abstraction; all that is here claimed is that it is not an "unreal" abstraction, but an identifiable constituent in experience.[45]

Lewis appears to be claiming that the contents of sensory consciousness, that is, the manifolds of sense whose constituents are observed qualia, consist of both thoughts as well as qualia. Qualia never come uninterpreted. But I do not find this claim to be plausible. When I see the red color that is presented in the appearance of an apple, I may very well be thinking 'That is red'. But the thought and its constitutive concepts are not objects of awareness but representations of objects of awareness. True, the observed color is part of a larger process extended in time and, as being part of a wider whole, may justly be termed an abstraction. In that sense, everything is an abstraction except the sum total of real being. What I see is the color. It is not something "excised"; its presence in my field of vision is not due to an act of thought. Whether or not I interpret it as red or interpret it in any way at all is an option that I may not choose to exercise. After all, the field of vision at any moment of time includes many more data than are actually interpreted at that time. What we interpret is usually that selection of data that our current concerns motivate us to attend to. To interpret is merely to think, and not every item in the field of consciousness is something we have a need to think about. (I will resume discussion of this issue later in this chapter.)

THE PROBLEM OF ACCESS

In the first section of this chapter, I reported one of the conclusions that G. E. Moore believed followed from his refutation of idealism: "There is, therefore, no question of how we are to 'get outside the circle of our own ideas and sensations.' Merely to have a sensation is already to *be* outside the circle. It is to know something which is as truly and really *not* a part of *my* experience, as anything which I can ever really know." However, our investigation has come to the contrary conclusion endorsed by Hume, who asserted that "all impressions are internal and perishing existences."[46]

There is, then, a genuine question of how we are to "get outside the circle of our own ideas and sensations." It has been answered already in my response to skepticism (in chapter 2): We have reliable procedures for discovering facts about nature, and these procedures often justify our beliefs and occasionally provide knowledge. We do not have to start with premises based upon our sensations; we can start anywhere. As Karl Popper has emphasized, inquiry is a matter of trial and error. Reliable procedures reveal error as well as provide a path to the truth.

This fact is illustrated by our discussion of the great deception of sense. Many of our beliefs about the location of sensory qualities are simply mistaken. Lemons are not yellow; tomatoes are not red; sounds do not travel through space. But because such beliefs are based upon sensory events that are related in a lawful way to events in the external world, they are useful and informative representations that we have no reason to jettison in our daily commerce with material objects. However, as philosophers, we want to know the truth of the matter, and have concluded that they are erroneous. The errors produced by the great deception of sense have been brought to light by the reliable procedures of theory construction in the sciences; this shows that even the framework of common sense may become an object of criticism and be revised in a provisional way in the course of inquiry. The sensory order does not, then, constitute *the* foundations of knowledge. There is no such thing as *the* foundations. Of course, the sensory order does constitute the basic input from the external world, but it is fallible and deceptive and can be reinterpreted in the light of theories that explain the nature and limitations of this input. Quine has spoken of "the meager input and the torrential output";[47] our beliefs transcend the specific information provided by the sensory order. Neither perception, induction, nor abduction are restricted to the specificities of our sensations. We are always operating within a provisional framework that represents an overall conception of the world; inquiry occurs within the framework and not only adds new items to its contents, but also occasionally stimulates us to construct major renovations. In the allegory of the cave, Plato claimed that reason is capable of leading us out of the cave into the sunlight so that we may grasp not merely images of the world, but the world as it really is. Inquiry is capable of transcending the cave or the framework of common sense; unfortunately, it produces a representation of a disenchanted world that makes the poets unhappy.

Inquiry can also be directed toward the study of our methods of fixing belief and can identify those that are reliable and those that are not, and it can also specify how reliable they are. We do this all the time in our everyday inquiries. I find that Jones' hearing is not as reliable as it once was; I discover that Smith's eyesight is not to be trusted; Edward's loss at poker shows that his estimates of probabilities are untrustworthy; and Cooper's prejudices make him an unreliable witness. In the same way, inquiry shows that the sensory order is unreliable when it comes to the ontology of the secondary qualities, although it can be relied upon when shopping for lemons.

REASONS AND CAUSES

In his discussion of the myth of the given in *Mind and World,* John McDowell explores the question of how the sensory order is capable of providing us with access to the world. In sense experience, the self, according to a common philosophical view, is receptive and, through various psychophysical processes, it is open to the input from the world. Once the input is received, the self applies its conceptual repertoire by means of which it can exercise its spontaneity in thinking about the world. Spontaneity is a kind of freedom of mind in which the self is not subject to blind causality but can look to the input to provide reasons for its beliefs, even though, as we saw, it is capable of transcending this meager input. It would appear, then, that receptivity exemplifies the causal order of psychophysical laws that produces sensory consciousness, whereas spontaneity introduces us to the realm of freedom in which thinking is under the control of reason and logic. But though the output is torrential, our beliefs and theories retain empirical significance as long as they remain vulnerable to the deliverances of experience.

But this way of looking at the matter generates the following problem. Receptivity belongs to the order of blind causality, but the data that are the products of receptivity interpreted in this way are not, according to McDowell, capable of providing reasons for our beliefs. They are not, as I have argued earlier, in propositional form, and, according to McDowell, they are not, therefore, capable of grounding premises for thought to work upon as it attempts to construct a justified representation of the world. "If experience plays only a causal role in the formation of a world-view, not a justificatory role, then it does not serve as evidence at all."[48]

One solution to this problem is the coherence theory of truth and knowledge, according to which empirical confirmation consists of epistemic and logical relations among beliefs triggered by sensory stimuli. But, according to McDowell, the coherence theory fails to explain how thinking is able to justify our representations of the world. For if all we have are logical and epistemic interconnections among beliefs, then we cannot understand how belief can be grounded in or be vulnerable to the deliverances of receptivity. Receptivity, understood as a process of blind causality, cannot justify a belief since it lacks propositional form. Experience is generally understood to provide access to the world, but it cannot do so if it is nothing more than a causally determined input. McDowell here adopts the Kantian idea that intuitions without concepts are blind, that is, they do not belong to the space of reasons.

McDowell's suggestion is to reject the idea that receptivity is a function of blind causality. The sensory order is already conceptualized; it provides glimpses of how things stand in the world. It does not merely trigger the activity of thought, as the coherence theory has it, but it provides direct access to the facts. Because it presents the world in conceptualized form, the sensory order presents us with materials that are capable of functioning as reasons and evidence for belief. What receptivity delivers already belongs to the space of reasons.

There are three main difficulties with this idea that the deliverances of receptivity are conceptualized. In the first place, the sensory order is subject to psychophysical laws. If, for example, a person is looking at a lemon in daylight and if there is nothing wrong with his eyes, he will see a yellow color. That is the working of blind causality. Of course, the psychophysical regularities are "designed" by natural selection to provide the type of input that enables the organism to survive. But the causality is blind in the sense that thinking plays no role in the formation of the regularities. There seems to be no room within receptivity, as understood in modern psychology, for conceptual formations to enter into the processes of the sensory order.[49]

In the second place, we have noted in previous discussions that sense perception is not propositional or conceptual in its very nature. It is not true that all seeing is seeing that, as McDowell claims. Although perceptual judgments occur in every moment of our waking life, they are products of our selective attention and current interests and needs and reflect activities of spontaneity rather than receptivity. Most of the input is not attended to at all; the self selects what it shall attend to; that is part of its freedom of mind.

Finally, although there is order in sense perception, it is not a conceptual order. When I look at something, I observe a structured visual scene, not a blooming buzzing confusion. I see relatively permanent objects arranged in space displaying colors and shapes; some are in the foreground and others in the background; their apparent colors are influenced by the circumambient light and the colors of their neighbors; movements and other events occur in a regular predictable manner. The order in the sensory order is, as the Gestalt psychologists have theorized, a product of the activity of the brain and nervous system. For example, the figure/ground relationship that pervades visual perception is totally involuntary and is not a product of thought or meaning.

Thus, although our intuitions are pre-conceptual and pre-propositional, they are not blind; they are ordered by neural/environmental interactions. Because they are ordered, it is possible for thought to ascribe concepts applicable to the items that appear, such as material substances, artifacts, and events. Moreover, among the items that appear are facts, not merely things. For example, I taste a sour lemon. Its being a sour lemon is something I perceive. I may not realize that it is a lemon I am tasting, and perhaps I may fail to classify its taste properly or even, because of illness, fail to sense its sourness, but that it is a sour lemon is accessible, ready to be represented in the proposition 'That lemon is sour' should I have some interest in formulating it.

Plato once claimed that if the objects of thought and experience are, as Heracleitus characterized them, like a flowing river into which one could not step twice, if the world were chaotic, a blooming, buzzing confusion, then knowledge would be impossible. That is why he postulated the Forms as stable elements that allow us to apply predicates to objects. In the same way, I suggest, thought can get a grip upon the material world through perception because the scenes apprehended exemplify various forms of order and repetition, allowing the self to use its linguistic and conceptual repertoire to represent how things stand in the objective world.

COLOR SKEPTICISM

In the discussion so far, I have argued that nothing material exemplifies color, that is, there are no colored material objects and events. The line of thought that has led to this conclusion has appeared to be moving in the direction of subjectivism, the idea that colors and other secondary qualities are mental entities. One way of interpreting subjectivism is to claim that there are mental entities that exemplify color, that is, that have properties described by color terms such as 'red', 'yellow', and so forth. Even if lemons are not yellow, the appearances of them are. The idea is that colors are subjectivized by being exported from the material world and imported into the mind. Colors reside in consciousness. That is one way of understanding the great deception of sense.

This understanding, however, cannot be correct as it stands. Whatever exemplifies color also exemplifies extension. Colored things occupy space. They are also visually discernible. On the subjectivist view, colored things are elements within the visual sensory manifold; they are embedded within the stream of consciousness. It is implausible to suppose that the stream of consciousness is itself unextended in the way required by subjectivism. On the view of the self identified with Descartes and Leibniz, the mind is unextended and cannot function as the locus of extended, colored things. On the physicalist view of the self, the mind is identified with the brain and states of consciousness with neural states. Colored things then would turn out to be extended colored patches discernible within the brain. But no such things have been found; what we do find are correlations between brain events and perceptions of color. Materialism is not consistent with the subjectivizing of the secondary qualities. When a person smells a skunk, the brain does not give off an unpleasant smell. When a loud noise is heard, the brain does not make a noise. The whole idea is absurd. One version of subjectivism is the idealism of Berkeley that has been refurbished as phenomenalism and neutral monism by philosophers who have thought that matter is reducible to sense data. However, these attempts are now generally thought to be failures, because none of the efforts at reduction have succeeded in capturing our conception of an independent material world. The idea that material objects are interpretable as logical constructions out of mental entities has gone by the wayside.

For these reasons, I want to propose a more radical version of the great deception of sense, called *color skepticism.* It asserts not merely that there are no colored material things, but that nothing whatsoever is colored at all. There are no colored material things; there are no colored mental things. It is true that many things seem to be colored, such as lemons and a mental image of a lemon. But that such appearances are deceptive, that nothing exemplifies color, is implied by the great deception of sense.

Having come to these conclusions, I am tempted to drop the subject. However, the position that things appear colored even though nothing at all exemplifies color seems to be so implausible to those who have considered the issue that I shall resist the temptation and venture to make some sense of it.

CONSCIOUSNESS AND COLOR

Let us start with the fact that lemons look yellow and tomatoes look red. It is a fact about the meaning of 'look' and other words designating the ways things appear that their use does not entail that anything is the way it appears. That this thing looks yellow or that thing looks red does not imply that this is yellow or that is red. Although there is a use in ordinary language in which color terms are predicated of sense experience, it does not imply that anything exemplifies color. I have used the term 'exemplification' as the name of the relation between a property and a thing that has that property. So the use of color terms as predicates of visual sense experience does not imply that these are predicated in the mode of exemplification.

One may wonder whether there are any other modes of predication. In order to show that there are, I want to point out a common misinterpretation of the thesis of color skepticism. The claim of color skepticism—that nothing exemplifies color—is frequently confused with color nihilism, according to which there are no colors. If one is a nominalist according to whom there are no unexemplified properties, then the former will be taken to imply the latter. But the color Platonist who allows for the reality of unexemplified properties will allow that there are colors even if nothing exemplifies them. And this makes it possible that there are modes of predication in addition to exemplification.

I will give two examples of such modes that may convince the doubters. Consider first a negative visual afterimage that is produced by staring for a few seconds at a bright light. If one then turns one's head toward a blank wall, one will usually see an image that bears a color that is complementary to the color of the light. Now there certainly is a state of consciousness that we call 'seeing an afterimage'. But there is no reason to suppose that there actually is a colored image that we see. It is, after all, a hallucination; we can verify that it is a hallucination by recalling the fact that no one else can see it. We readily describe our experience of afterimages using color terms, but quickly realize upon reflection that there is nothing there except a state of consciousness that appears to, but does not really, exemplify color. Second, imagine a bright red tomato. You are seeing in your mind's eye something to which you are inclined to apply the predicate 'red', but you also realize that there is nothing there except the state of consciousness that we describe as imagining a red tomato. This is a case in which we would agree both that the act of imagining is best described using the term 'red tomato' and that there is nothing really red there. In one way there is nothing mysterious here; perhaps something is going on in one's brain that resembles what goes on when one sees a real tomato. Of course, as a matter of fact, we directly produce the image through an act of will, so we might be inclined to say that the image causes the brain event, whereas in the case of the afterimage we might be inclined to claim that the brain event causes the image. But whatever the direction of causation, it is plausible on the basis of what we already know about psychophysics to suppose that there are correlations that enter into a causal explanation of either the occurrences of images or the occurrences of brain processes.

What is mysterious is how color enters into the experience of these images, whether they are afterimages or direct products of the imagination. I suggest that we posit another type of predication, in which properties are ascribed to various occurrences. I shall label it 'predication in the mode of illustration'; a quale that is embedded in sensory consciousness shall be said to be illustrated by a state of consciousness. It should be understood that the item to which a predicate in the mode of illustration is applied does not exemplify the property so predicated; states of consciousness are capable of reaching out, so to speak, to abstract objects such as properties without any implication that these states actually exemplify them.

I suggest that colors and other qualia enter into perceptual and sensory experiences in the mode of illustration. Lemons look yellow and yellow is embedded in their looking yellow, yet neither the lemons nor the state of consciousness that we describe as an instance of looking yellow are actually yellow.

I do not claim any originality at all for this idea. Around 1920 a group of philosophers who wrote under the banner of critical realism published a collection of their essays entitled *Essays in Critical Realism.* One of the contributors was George Santayana, who states: "sensible . . . essences are the apparent qualities of the thing perceived."[50] He explains what he means by 'essence' as follows: "By 'essence' I understand a universal, of any degree of complexity and definition, which may be given immediately whether to sense or thought." And just in case he should be misunderstood, he adds: "the datum is not an existing thing, nor a state of mind, but an ideal essence."[51] Another contributor was Durant Drake, who claims: "the datum is, *qua* datum, a mere essence, an imputed but not necessarily actual existent. It may or may not have existence."[52] In the same book, C. A. Strong asserts: "the datum is a mere essence, a universal."[53]

The critical realists were employing the ancient distinction between essence and existence. Essences are universals, abstract objects capable of exemplification but not necessarily exemplified. Existing things, on the other hand, are concrete realities capable of exemplifying essences. Essences do not exist in the sense of being concrete realities in space and time. But they are not nothing either. The category of essence is indispensable for a full account of the nature of reality, and therefore essences can be listed among the real things. This is a version of Plato's theory of Forms, and, when applied to color, may justly be labeled 'color Platonism'. In fact, the discussion in this section is an argument in favor of color Platonism and against nominalism, because it claims that qualia are universals or essences that have an indispensable role in explaining sensory consciousness. The sensory manifold of which we are directly aware is a complex, constantly changing, ephemeral state of consciousness illustrated by a pattern of qualia whose structure and organization are determined by the program of the brain "designed" by natural selection. Berkeley's claim that the *esse* of ideas is *percipi* is true of sensory manifolds; they exist only as objects of sensory consciousness. A sensory manifold is composed of states of consciousness, particulars that illustrate qualia. The qualia themselves, however, are abstract objects whose status is not restricted to the particulars that have illustrated them but are capable of being illustrated repeatedly by future particulars.

One may object that I have fallen into a serious contradiction. I have provided arguments to show that the sensory manifold is not itself conceptualized, and that conceptualization is a product of the perceptual judgment that applies predicates to objects. But now I am claiming that qualia are abstract objects—universals. Are not universals the same thing as concepts? But the contradiction is apparent, not real. Call universals concepts if you will; that does not imply that the manifold of sense is already conceptualized in the sense of being a product of thought as well as sense. Seeing *that* such and such is so involves an act of conceptualization, but the simple seeing *of* such and such does not, even if universals are exemplified or illustrated by its objects.

ADVERBS AND ADJECTIVES

There is another account of the nature of sensory consciousness, called the adverbial theory, according to which terms for qualia should by interpreted not as adjectives predicated in some mode or other of states of consciousness but as adverbs predicated of a manner of sensing. On the adverbial theory, the statement that a lemon looks yellow to me should be interpreted as saying that in seeing the lemon, I am sensing yellowly. Adjectives are converted into adverbs that represent adverbial properties of sensory states of consciousness. One advantage claimed for the adverbial approach is that it no longer conceives states of consciousness as if they exemplified properties of material objects. To say that something looks red and square to someone means that he is sensing redly and squarely; these are manners, not objects, of sense awareness. Thus one avoids the difficulties of Locke's resemblance theory that predicates certain properties—the primary qualities—of both ideas and bodies in the same mode. It avoids, it is claimed, reifying states of consciousness as if they are inner replicas of physical things. One cannot say of an idea that it is square in the same sense that the body perceived is square. Another advantage claimed for it is that it avoids Moore's problem of being confined to the circle of ideas. Since ideas are merely manners of sensing, one is in direct contact with the external world. The existence of the external world is not the conclusion of a shaky inference, but is given directly in sense perception.

No doubt these are reasons in favor of the adverbial theory, but there are significant objections to it that convince me that it is incorrect. First, colors are things seen, that is, they are objects to a subject; on this descriptive or phenomenological interpretation, sensory manifolds including imagined scenes are objects of awareness, not manners of awareness (whatever that means). In addition, as I pointed out earlier, they are highly organized objects of awareness; one thing is seen as being in front of another; one sound is heard at a distance and another is heard as coming from the right. Qualia are presented as illustrating various modes of togetherness, as when the same thing illustrates different qualities in different ways. This phenomenology is consistent both with theories of illustration and exemplification but is difficult to make sense of on the adverbial account.

In the second place, I have pointed out several times that there is no semantic duality in color terms. In 'The lemon is yellow' and 'The lemon looks yellow', the term 'yellow' occurs with the same meaning. In veridical perception, the color that it looks to have is the same as the color that it does have. But this identity of color is incompatible with the adverbial theory because the latter claims that there is a semantic duality: 'yellow' as applied to the lemon names a property ascribed to a body, but as applied to the appearance it names a manner of sensing.

An advocate of the adverbial theory may try to shake this objection off. He may admit that in our ordinary speech there is no semantic duality, but argue that ordinary speech is misleading because the absence of a duality leads to a theory of sense awareness that produces insoluble problems. It is better to admit that this transformation of adjectives and nouns into adverbs is not intended as an explication of the ordinary meaning of color terms; rather, it replaces the ordinary meaning when it occurs in appearance statements by a new concept that is less problematic. However, in reply to this defense, I must point out that the adverbial theory has an intractable problem of its own, namely, its inconsistency with the phenomenology of sense awareness.

This leads to the third objection. We say that appearances are sometimes correct or veridical and sometimes mistaken. They are correct when, for example, the thing that looks rectangular is rectangular, and incorrect when the thing that looks rectangular is not rectangular. Things sometimes look the way they are: this is what Locke was getting at with his resemblance hypothesis. The critical realists used this fact to explain how perception can be a source of both knowledge and error. C. A. Strong formulates the issue as follows:

> If the essence is truly the essence of the object, as it should be in order that knowledge may be correct, the essence given and the essence embodied are not two but one . . . the datum is a mere essence, a universal. . . . It is precisely because it is a mere universal that the essence given and the essence embodied in the object may be the same, and that the mind in sense-perception may therefore be able to rest directly on the object.[54]

> Error of perception . . . is possible only because the givenness of the essence is independent of its embodiment, in such a wise that an essence may be given different to a greater or lesser extent from that which is embodied. . . . Truth of perception is possible only because the essences given are not existences, but universals, the bare natures . . . of the objects, in such wise that the essence embodied and the essence given may be the same.[55]

In these passages we see a suggestion of an identity theory of truth. Perception provides the basis for true perceptual judgments when the qualia illustrated are identical with the qualities exemplified. Judgment in general is true when the possible state of affairs asserted to exist is identical with one that does exist. In this way, there is no circle of ideas to break out of because of the identity between idea and object.

But the adverbial theory cannot appeal to identity to explain how perceptual truth is possible, since it postulates that 'red' and 'redly' name different features. Nor can it explain occasional error. Suppose something that is red looks orange in this light. We would say in this case that the experience is misleading, since it looks different from what it is. But on the adverbial theory, the appearances are always misleading because the way something looks can never be the same as the way it is. We need a theory to explain both truth and error, and the adverbial theory makes sense of neither. Of course, color skepticism agrees with the adverbial theory that appearances are characteristically misleading, but it explains how they are misleading in a way compatible with the possibility of error and in accord with the phenomenology of sense experience.

The view of perception in this chapter is consistent with the argument of Leibniz's mill. We do not find perception as we stroll through the brain because, amidst the roar of physical processes occurring within and among the neurons, we do not find sensory manifolds illustrating qualia. Sense awareness becomes accessible only to an introspective first-person point of view. But we do not find the person in the brain, either, nor do we find the mechanism that provides any explanation of how these experiences are *my* experiences. On the view of the self of Descartes and Leibniz, we do find sense perception as we stroll through the self because the only way one can stroll through it is to *be* it, and in that case, sense awareness is introspectively accessible.

Chapter Five

AGENCY

THE STRUCTURE OF HUMAN ACTION

Consider this situation. A visitor observes that X is standing in his garden with a shovel in his hand. "What are you doing?" he asks. X replies, "I am digging a hole in order to plant a tree." The surface logical form that his reply illustrates is: (1) 'X does A in order to G' where 'X' names the *agent,* 'A' designates what he is doing, or, as I shall call it from now on, his *action,* and 'G' designates his *goal* or aim or purpose in doing it. If the action is successful in the agent's intention to produce G, then 'G' names not only the intended goal but also the actual result achieved. I take (1) to represent the typical form of goal-directed action. Although it is somewhat artificial to divide an instance of human behavior into an action and a goal component because the goal is often mentioned in describing the action itself, it is useful for the discussion that follows to distinguish these two components in this way. Actions are susceptible of a variety of different descriptions depending upon the context and purpose of description; conditions that would be listed in some contexts as results or intended results would, in other contexts, be included as parts of the action itself.

Not all human conduct appears to be goal-directed. Some things are done for their own sake, as when one listens to music for the enjoyment of it rather than with the aim of bringing about some result. But even things done for their own sake may often be analyzable into an action and goal: the action is listening to the music, and the goal is the pleasure derived from it. After all, the pleasure may be hoped for but fail to occur, and, therefore, it is distinguishable from the action of just listening. So I shall focus on goal-directed conduct as the paradigmatic case of human action.

An action is something done on purpose. So accidents, reflex responses, involuntary movements, and so forth are not, in this technical sense, human actions. I do not exclude some animals as performing actions if what they do is genuinely goal-directed. But I do exclude the movements of nonliving mechanisms. Consider a missile aimed at a certain target where the flight of the missile is controlled by feedback mechanisms that keep it on course. It is not uncommon to describe its flight as goal-directed because of the operation of the feedback mechanism. Feedback also occurs in human action and is indispensable in getting things done. But the missile's flight is not something that it does intentionally or on purpose or with the intention of hitting the target. The missile has no mind and thus has no intentions or ends in view. A person who is doing something on purpose has an *idea in mind* of what he is trying to accomplish; this is his *end in view,* and it is a constituent of his having just that intention. Human action essentially involves intentionality; it incorporates a form of representational or referential consciousness that functions to guide the agent's movements to a successful outcome.

The action A is often characterized as a *means* to G, and G is characterized as the *intended result* of A. Thus getting the tree planted is the intended result of digging the hole. If the action is successful—the hole is actually dug and the tree planted—then G is the *actual result* of A. Of course, A will have many other consequences: the tree will grow, X will hurt his back, and so on, but I shall limit the term 'result' to the realized goal that is intended and classify the other outcomes as *consequences.*

It is common to characterize the relation between means and ends or results as instances of cause and effect. But it is not correct to say that the dug hole is the cause of the tree being planted. The tree's being planted is the result of a sequence of planned events and realized conditions, not all of which are aptly described as causes. For example, purchasing the fertilizer and transporting it to the garden are among these events but would hardly be thought of as causes. They themselves are actions. I shall describe the situation in these terms: In doing A in order to G, X has G in mind as his end in view; in thinking about how he shall accomplish G, he forms a *plan* involving a sequence of factors; some of these factors are conditions to be achieved, such as the hole being dug; others are actions such as buying the fertilizer and bringing it to the garden; others are events such as the automobile starting up on the return trip from the garden shop. The plan includes all and only the factors the agent consciously includes within it, although many things can happen along the way that he does not think of and that are not part of the plan. This intended sequence of factors, the totality of conceived means to the end G, is X's *envisaged path.* Should the plan be completely successful, then the intended sequence is an actual sequence, the envisaged path is an *actual path,* and G is the actual result. Even if the path comes into existence as envisaged, the plan may not be successful, and G may fail to occur. As time passes, the plan may be modified to take into account unforeseen difficulties.

AGENT AND SPECTATOR

The agent's point of view is directed to the future, for that is when the goal will be realized. In *deliberation,* he reflects both on the goal to be chosen and the path to achieve it. Once he identifies his goal—planting a tree on this spot—he forms a plan to get it done. He is concerned with the link between the envisaged path P and G. Will P succeed in bringing about G? Is P with its various factors, including his digging a hole, sufficient to get the tree planted? Is this plan better than that in terms of efficiency, cost, risk, chance of success, opportunities forgone, and so forth? If X is asked to explain why he is digging a hole, he will refer to G as his *reason* for doing A. G is his end in view, and X has adopted A as part of his plan because he believes it is the best way to bring about this result. Because of the intended link between A and G, he explains his doing A by reference to G. Of course, because G lies in the future and may never in fact come into existence, the claim that he does A because of G is clearly not a statement of cause and effect. The *because* in this context is not a causal concept. G cannot be the cause of A because G lies in A's future. Even if the plan in some sense causes or, better yet, is a means to the result, the result cannot be the cause of the planned action. The explanation that X offers of why he is doing A is not a causal explanation, for the future does not cause the past, but a *teleological explanation,* a way of understanding actions in terms of the envisaged result.

The disinterested spectator, on the other hand, does not have G as his goal, and he is not involved in making a decision. As an observer, he is occupied in observing what X does rather than exercising his own will in making a choice. He recognizes that the plan may misfire and G may never be achieved. Thus, when X tells him that the reason why he is digging a hole is in order to plant a tree on this spot, he understands what X says not only as a teleological explanation by reference to G but as an explanation that makes reference to the idea of G in X's mind, for it is this idea of G that constitutes X's end in view that guides his actions. Since the idea of G exists prior to A, it would appear that for the spectator the basic explanation is causal. The spectator understands the phrase *in order to* to have implicit reference not only to G but to the idea of G; this idea is what gets X's feet to move; it is the basis of his predicting what X will do.

REASONS

The agent X mentions G as his reason for digging the hole. A reason R in this context is something intended, a future occurrence that may or may not come into existence depending upon how successful the plan is. R (that is, G as intended) is classified as a reason because it not only explains why X is doing A but also justifies or makes sense of what he is doing. A spectator who is interested in evaluating X's conduct may want to know X's reasons for what he is doing in order to determine whether or not he is rational. An action is rational to the extent to which the reason why it is being done is a good reason; there are so many potential factors involved in a reason's being good or bad—prudential, ethical, technical, and so on—that they cannot be specified here. I am here speaking of practical reason, the way reason is embedded not merely in thought but also in action.

The envisaged results lie in the future. So reasons themselves, the intended consequences, cannot be the causes of X's action. We must distinguish the reason R from the fact that it is intended. The term 'R' refers to the envisaged result and alludes to the fact of its being intended. R is subsequent to the action, whereas the fact that it is intended antedates it.

I have labeled that fact the end in view, the idea in mind, the envisaged goal, and so forth. This involves a representation in X's mind of G, together with representations of elements of the plan as it becomes clear to X what he must do to realize G. When, in deliberation, X forms his plan of action, P, he comes to believe that P is the best means to bringing G into existence. Underlying his deliberation is the fact that he has a favorable attitude toward G relative to the rejected alternatives: why else would he take the trouble to bring it into existence? When X has finished deliberating about what he shall do, there exists in his mind a complex representational and affective state that has as its components his belief that P will succeed in bringing about G, his intention to bring about G, his intention to bring about the elements of P as the means to bring about G, his desire for or favorable attitude toward G and to the plan, P, that he hopes will bring it about. I shall call this type of complex mental state a *teleological frame of mind* (TFM). It includes a structured array of beliefs, intentions, desires, and emotions. An agent's TFM constitutes his *complete end in view.* Should X act in the light of his TFM, what he does is *voluntary* and *freely chosen.*

It is not at all uncommon in modern thought about human conduct to think of what people do as being explicable in causal terms. A related thought is that there are sufficient causal conditions for all voluntary actions. Even though teleological explanation is not reducible to causal explanation, they are, it is claimed, compatible with one another. There is no conflict between interpreting a person's behavior teleologically in the light of his goals and causally by reference to the states of mind that get his feet to move. One who adopts this point of view is committed to the idea that an action can be both free and caused at the same time. This idea, sometimes called *compatibilism,* has been advocated in different versions by such luminaries as Hobbes, Hume, and Kant. A compatibilist who is also a physicalist would claim that the TFM of any agent is to be identified with processes and dispositions of the brain and nervous system. Human action belongs to the order of nature and can be understood in physical terms.

I think this way of thinking is mistaken and is founded in modern times upon an erroneous appeal to science. In what follows, I shall suggest an alternative account that provides a more plausible interpretation of human freedom.

DELIBERATION, DESIRE, AND WILL

We deliberate about both ends and means. Deliberation is future-oriented and occurs when there is some doubt about what shall be done. X thinks: Should I plant a tree here or leave the grass to grow? He wants a tree more than the bare grass and then thinks whether or not he should dig the hole himself or hire someone else to do it. What is to be done? How shall it be done? These are the questions facing practical reason in the context of decision. Deliberation proceeds until the agent has made a decision that selects one among the alternatives that structure the practical problem he faces. The direct result of deliberation is a teleological frame of mind such that, unless he changes his mind, he will, at the appropriate time, proceed to act so that his envisioned goal will be realized in accordance with the plan he has settled upon.

In chapter 6 of *Leviathan,* Thomas Hobbes offers the following account of deliberation:

> When in the mind of man, Appetites, and Aversions, Hopes, and Feares, concerning one and the same thing, arise alternately; and divers good and evill consequences of the doing, or omitting the thing propounded, come successively into our thoughts; so that sometimes we have an Appetite to it; sometimes an Aversion from it; sometimes Hope to be able to do it; sometimes Despaire, or Feare to attempt to do it; the whole summe of Desires, Aversions, Hopes and Fears, continued till the thing be either done, or thought impossible, is what we call DELIBERATION. . . . In *Deliberation,* the last Appetite, or Aversion, immediately adhering to the action, or to the omission thereof, is what wee call the WILL; the Act, (not the faculty,) of *Willing. . . . Will* therefore *is the last Appetite in Deliberating.*[1]

For Hobbes, deliberation consists of a succession of desires, or, as he terms them, appetites and aversions, together with evaluative thoughts about the consequences of the actions being considered. His description of deliberation represents it as a mechanical process, as if deliberating were not something under the control of the agent. For him, desires just arise, one after the other. The choice or act of will is interpreted by Hobbes to be the desire that immediately precedes the action. In deliberation, there is a sequence of subjective states—desires and thoughts—and, at a certain point, the sequence comes to an end and the agent acts. Notice the suggestion of passivity in this account: Desires "arise alternatively"; the good and evil consequences "come successively into our thoughts"; the act "proceedeth from the *Will.*" It is if the agent were simply a machine going through a series of internal states.

Hobbes' description of the deliberative process neglects the fact that the agent, in trying to make up his mind what to do, embarks upon an active, searching process. Deliberation is not just a sequence of internal states but a series of actions to a great extent under the control of the agent. The will, by which I mean the agent's capacity for choice and decision, is active throughout the deliberative process. Moreover, the decision to do this rather than that is not, as Hobbes claims, just another desire, even the final desire that precedes the action. When X concludes that he prefers to have a tree in that spot rather than plain grass, he then forms the intention or chooses to adopt that goal and to implement the plan. It is the forming of the intention, the making of the choice, the coming to a decision that is properly construed as an act of will. Willing is not reducible to desire.[2] A desire is not an intention or an end in view. The terminus of deliberation is a teleological frame of mind that includes desires but intentions as well. To desire this is not yet to choose this. To want that is not yet to have made up one's mind to pursue it as a goal. The teleological frame of mind is itself the outcome of the agent's act of deciding upon one course of action rather than another. We should think of the will as that function of the self that is both legislature and executive. The legislative function declares what the goal is and settles on a plan of action to carry it out. The executive function implements the decision by carrying out the plan and monitoring the results in order to stay on the right path.[3] The body and its machinery do not deliberate and decide but serve as the self's instrument by means of which the 'I' is effective in the spatiotemporal physical world. Desires are analogous to special interests that importune the self to opt for this and that alternative. While we are developing this metaphor, let us not neglect the judicial function of the self that reviews the course of action, judges it to be well or ill done, offers congratulations for a job well done or regrets for failure, and considers what steps to take next. The capacity to feel regret, along with the pangs of conscience,[4] is the emotional representation of failure; it is the ability of the self to understand that it should have done otherwise and implies that it could have done otherwise. In case we are tempted to fall into self-deception or, in Sartre's terms, bad faith, regret reminds us of our freedom and responsibility.

A desire is not an act of will. It is an attitude that favors some outcome. Deliberation occurs because there is a conflict of attitudes: X likes the grass in that spot but would also enjoy having a tree there. Because the minds of persons are filled with appetites and aversions, the world is not a neutral place, a collection of objects that are just there. Objects are apprehended in relation to desires and emotions; they are pleasing or disliked, loved or feared. People apprehend the objects that surround them as things that can affect them for good or ill. In addition, a person's desires structure the range of alternatives from which he chooses. In deliberation, not every abstract possibility is relevant; desires and other attitudes direct the agent's attention, influence the course of deliberation, and narrow his horizon of possibilities.[5] Of course, the term 'desire' is too narrow to encompass all the attitudes and beliefs that structure the options facing an agent. An action may be thought to be legally or morally obligatory or virtuous or prudent or useful or desirable. Such evaluations contribute to structuring the range of alternatives.

In short, desires and other attitudes and beliefs set the stage for deliberation. They determine the opening scene. But how the drama proceeds from there is up to the agent. In deliberation, he must decide what weight to give to the attitudes that create his problem in the first place. He solves the problem by determining his goals, rejecting alternatives, and settling upon a plan. In his acts of will, he projects himself into the future in a direction that frequently cannot be predicted on the basis of the opening scene. As the play begins, the script for the scenes that follow is yet to be written.

REASONS AND CAUSES

How shall we understand the relation between the reason for an action and the action? What is the relation between X's desire to have a tree planted in that spot and his digging the hole? I suggested that reasons often serve to justify actions. Donald Davidson has claimed that something more is involved. "But suppose we grant that reasons alone justify in explaining actions: it does not follow that the explanation is not also causal." Indeed, giving reasons is also "a species of causal explanation."[6]

Davidson points out that "a person can have a reason for an action, and perform the action, and yet this reason not be the reason why he did it. Central to the relation between a reason and an action it explains is the idea that the agent performed the action *because* he had the reason."[7] How shall we interpret the 'because'? Davidson answers: "One way we can explain an event is by placing it in the context of its cause; cause and effect form the sort of pattern that explains the effect, in a sense of 'explain' that we understand as well as any. If reason and action illustrate a different pattern of explanation, that pattern must be identified."[8] The best argument in favor of the causal interpretation is "that it alone promises to give an account of the 'mysterious connection' between reasons and actions."[9]

I have already noted that this formulation of the problem is unsatisfactory. Reasons in the cases I have specified cannot be the causes of actions because they are subsequent to them. The 'because' that ties reasons or goals to human conduct represents teleological explanation: X did A *because* of G, that is, *in order to* bring about G. Teleological explanation is not causal. It does not provide an antecedent condition that makes something happen, but explains why it happened in the sense of what the agent was aiming at. When we speak of the strength of a reason, we are not referring to a psychophysical force it is alleged to possess but rather to its logical powers, to how well the agent believes that it serves to justify the action being considered.

A teleological frame of mind is the mental outcome of the agent's deliberative process. It contains the end in view in the form of facts of intending and of having various goals and plans in mind. It includes desires, emotions, and other attitudes. It also precedes that action, and thus is the most likely candidate for a causal condition, if anything is. So the thesis that the reason why an agent acted as he did is the cause (or a cause) of what he did should be reformulated as the claim that the agent's teleological frame of mind or some element therein such as his desire is the cause of his action.

CAUSALITY AND COMPULSION

The items that enter into a teleological frame of mind, however, are not good candidates for functioning as causal conditions of action. Suppose a man is convicted of a burglary; the judge is about to sentence him and asks the offender if there is anything he wants to say. The burglar replies: "Your honor, I have an excuse; I wanted the jewels hidden in that house; that is why I formed the intention of breaking into it; my wanting them and my intention made me do it. I really had no choice in the matter." The judge, of course, would think that this was a joke. The fact that the offender wanted the jewels did not force his hand, make him do it, or necessitate that he break into the house. To use an expression of Leibniz, the thief's desires incline without necessitating. After all, if his teleological frame of mind made him do it, he would have an excuse sufficient to exonerate him. Instead, the judge would say to him: "You had the power and the ability to choose not to give in to your desires. There was no cause either external or internal forcing you to become a thief. You could have done otherwise. You have no excuse at all."[10]

The usual reply offered by the compatibilist to this argument starts by distinguishing between causation in general and compulsion. A person is compelled to do A if he is forced to act *contrary* to his desires. The thief threatens: "Your money or your life." Since his victim prefers to live, he hands over his wallet even though he does not want to. That is compulsion. Desires as such do not compel, but that does not disqualify them from being causes. Because the burglar's teleological frame of mind did not compel him to break the law, he had no excuse. But that does not entail that it did not cause him to break the law. Compulsion sometimes provides an excuse; merely wanting something does not.

I think this argument about the nature of the causal connection is mistaken. It rests ultimately on the view that causality consists of constant conjunction or correlation between events or conditions. However, this analysis of the causal tie is implausible because there are cases of correlation that are not cases of causal connection. The history of discussion about the nature of causality tends to show that our ordinary concept of causality cannot be reduced to correlation. When we search for causes, we want to identify conditions and events that make something happen.

Moreover, in the indeterministic universe that modern physics claims to be our universe, constant conjunctions are not necessary for causal connections at all. In fact, we are quite good at spotting causality even in the absence of lawful constancies. Our ability to know what causes what in the events of everyday life outruns our knowledge of the laws of nature. A cause is something that makes something else happen. Causes compel. The burglar was not compelled to his life of crime, and therefore the excuse he offered was no excuse at all. When we speak of a person being forced to do something against his will, we are referring to a felt compulsion, where the power of the cause enters into his consciousness. But events can compel other events without anyone being conscious of that fact. The fire made the tree burn down; the force of the flood made the dikes crumble; the light made my eyes blink.[11] I do not offer these remarks as a definition of the concept of causality. I think that this is such a fundamental category that there can be no perspicuous analysis of it.

Those who adopt a deterministic model of human motivation would analyze the judge's claim that the burglar could have done otherwise to mean that if he had different desires, then he would have done otherwise. Now, it may be true that he would have done otherwise if his desires had been different. But what the judge means is that even if his desires had remained the same, it was in his power to resist temptation. The reason it was in his power is that his desires do not constitute sufficient causal conditions; his desires inclined him to certain actions without necessitating that he perform them. The fact that his desires remained the same does not entail that he could not act otherwise. He had the power to do so because desires do not make him act. They do not force his hand. What he does is up to him. His desires structure his options; they do not cause him to act.

I do not want to deny that there are irresistible impulses. A person may be addicted to a certain drug so that the pain caused by his not taking it is so intense as to make it impossible for him to resist temptation. In that case, he is no longer in control of his conduct; he lacks the power to do otherwise, and thus he may have a valid excuse. However, irresistible impulses are not the typical or normal desires. The error of compatibilism is to take irresistible impulses as the model for desires generally. Whether or not a desire is irresistible is something to be determined on empirical grounds; that a desire inclines without necessitating is also verifiable on empirical grounds. Compatibilism appears to me to be empirically falsified.

THE MYSTERIOUS CONNECTION

Davidson is correct in distinguishing between an agent's reasons for action and the reason why he acted. X may have a reason for doing A, but he may end up doing A for a reason different from the one he originally considered. The actual reason he has for his action is his *motivating reason* (M). X wants to plant a tree in that spot; that is what motivates him to dig a hole there. Perhaps he originally thought of digging a hole there because he thought that he needed a well in the vicinity. But he changed his mind; wanting the tree in the spot is what actually motivated him to start digging.

In the process of deliberation, X first decides he would like a tree there and then decides to dig a hole himself. What makes M into a motivating reason is the fact that he chose that course of action for that reason. X decides to dig the hole because he decides in favor of placing a tree there. His making that decision is what makes his wanting a tree there his motivating reason for digging the hole. Of all the things he could do, he concludes that planting a tree there is the one he wants most and that digging the hole himself is the plan that will achieve his goal most efficiently.

Let me formulate the outcome of this analysis in terms that may strike us as paradoxical: *We choose our own motives.* It seems paradoxical because the term 'motive' suggests causation, a moving cause.[12] But in actual fact, the process of deliberation includes as an essential moment the determination in thought of the reason that has the greatest weight; this is the reason that becomes the motive.[13] The agent is thinking about the best thing for him to do; his deciding what is best not only leads him to act as he does but also leads him to make up his mind why he should act as he does. Why he acts as he does is his motivating reason. We choose not only what we do but also why we do what we do; in choosing what to do, agents thereby choose the "why." The transformation of an agent's reason for an action into the reason why he acted as he did is accomplished by his will. The agent's decision transforms a reason for action into an effective reason that guides his subsequent conduct.

I suggested, in agreement with Davidson, that reasons usually serve to justify. X thinks himself justified in digging a hole there because that is where he will plant a tree. Digging a hole there is, in his mind, the best thing for him to be doing now. That is what he prefers. Of course he could be mistaken. Perhaps it is more important at this time to change the oil in his auto engine or to shop for the party he is giving. He could have made the wrong choice in the light of all his present needs and commitments. In that case, he is not justified in digging the hole. That he wants a tree there explains why he is digging a hole, but that is not the best way for him to spend his time. So motivating reasons do not always succeed in justifying, although the agent thinks that they do so. His thinking that they do so is what inclines him to choose this action and thus make these desires his motivating reasons. The mysterious connection between reasons and actions is the act of choice, of deciding to do this rather than that.

Sometimes we use the term 'motive' in a different way when we want to delve deeper into the agent's mind in order to explain why he decided to do this rather than that, where what we are after is something that explains the attraction of his motivating reason. Why does X want a tree there? Because he is vain about the look of his garden and wants to have a better garden than his neighbors. His horticultural vanity explains why he finds it so urgent to plant a tree there now. In this usage, a motive is a character trait expressed in action; it represents an orientation of the agent's personality. It goes beyond what belongs to the consciousness of the agent and points to factors that he may not recognize himself. But vanity is not a cause; it does not compel or force him to act; the ascription of vanity interprets what he does in the light of a disposition of character that inclines him to pursue certain types of goals.[14] We can even go further and ask for the source of his horticultural vanity. Why does he care so much about having the best garden? At this point we are raising questions about his past activities, successes, competitive spirit, and the like.

THE WILL AND THE BRAIN

Where, then, are we to find the causes of X's action? The physicalist replies that they are among the events in his brain. His ends in view, his teleological frame of mind, and his motivating reasons are actually aspects of or features of events in his brain. Thus, sufficient causal conditions are to be found, not by introspection, but by study of what happens in the brain that leads to action.

We have already presented reasons to believe that the functions of the self that exemplify intentionality are not reducible to purely physical states of the brain. Perhaps they are irreducibly mental aspects of brain events. This would be a kind of halfway house between physicalistic reductionism and Cartesian dualism. But we have seen that, with the exception of irresistible impulses, intentional states of consciousness are not candidates for being causal conditions of human conduct. So if the brain does it all, then the argument requires that the constituents of the teleological frame of mind are merely epiphenomena that accompany the brain processes that exemplify them, but that play no role in the act of choice. They are mere passive reflections of purely physical processes.

But then, I think, the physicalist is required to conclude that human conduct does not really issue from acts of choice. It is a direct product of what goes on in the brain. In that case, we must deny that there is anything going on that can be entitled an act of choice or decision. When X decides to dig a hole and then does it, his action appears to issue from his decision. But if it actually issued from non-intentional aspects of his brain, then he didn't really decide or choose even if it seems to him that he did. Just like radical physicalism, this halfway house between physicalism and Cartesian dualism must reject the reality of the human will. Our self-interpretation that brings the will into play as producing our actions is an illusion. The introspective first-person point of view is an inaccurate guide to the understanding of human conduct.

The problem with this halfway house is that it is empirically false. All the evidence points to the fact that human beings really do deliberate, choose, make decisions, and then act to make their decisions effective. The self cannot be identified with the brain, nor can its actions be identified with brain processes. Human experience supports the reality of the will and points in the direction of an active self along the lines Descartes advocated.

In response, the physicalist might claim that just as there is, in Hobbes' terms, a great deception of sense, so there is a great deception of introspection. The introspective evidence is not conclusive and can be outweighed by scientific considerations. And science, it might be claimed, supports determinism and physicalism.

SCIENCE AND FREE WILL

In medieval and early modern philosophy the debate about free will often centered around theological issues: If God is responsible for everything that happens and if he knows ahead of time everything that anyone will do, then it is doubtful that there is anything that can be called freedom of action and moral responsibility. With the rise of modern science, the question shifted to the implications of physical science for human conduct. Newton's representation of nature popularized deterministic models of natural happenings in which there seemed no room for the type of free will advocated by Descartes, who said: "I know by experience that it [the will or freedom of choice] is not restricted in any way."[15] According to Laplace in the early nineteenth century, "we ought then to regard the present state of the universe as the effect of its anterior state and as the cause of the one which is to follow."[16] Davidson formulates this understanding in terms of the idea of law: "where there is causality, there must be a law; events related as cause and effect fall under strict deterministic laws."[17] From the idea that nature is governed by strict deterministic laws arose such doctrines as hard determinism, according to which there is no such thing as free will, and soft determinism, which implies the compatibility of freedom and causation.[18]

The rise of quantum physics in the twentieth century has made it clear that physical science is not inherently deterministic. The scientific knowledge available at any given time consists of an organized body of theories and conjectures supported by experience and elaborated in accordance with logical principles. There is no reason a priori to suppose that physical science must be either deterministic or indeterministic. In its present phase, science is indeterministic. The laws of nature should not be assumed to take a deterministic form but rather, as Peirce and Whitehead have suggested, should be thought of as analogous to habits that may be more or less rigid as experience tells us. In the light of the recent revolution in our understanding of nature, Patrick Suppes claims "that the probabilistic character of temporal phenomena is almost as ubiquitous as their spatial or temporal character."[19] He adds "that the occurrences of randomness in nature are legion . . . the universe is essentially probabilistic in character . . . the world is full of random happenings."[20] Moreover, our ascriptions of probability are not due to ignorance. "It is not just the quantum world that has an essential random component—it is almost every aspect of experience. The evidence supports the thesis that random or probabilistic phenomena are found in nature and not simply in our lack of knowledge."[21]

The probabilistic understanding of nature should not, of course, be identified with free will.[22] Rather, indeterminacy makes room for the efficacy of deliberation and choice, and it undermines the efforts of advocates of strict laws of nature to deny freedom and responsibility. Freedom of action is not to be identified with randomness; just the opposite. To the extent to which deliberation and choice are effective, a person's conduct is under his control; he is thus responsible for what he does because he could have done otherwise.

Not only is science not inherently deterministic in its conception of the course of nature, it is not inherently physicalistic or materialistic. The only metaphysical constraint upon science is that the existence of whatever entities, conditions, and laws are implied by its theories must be supported by experience and logic. There is no general argument based upon the nature of science that calls into question either the existence of a self that is not reducible to its physical conditions or the reality of the will, that is, the reality of that function of the self involved in deliberation and choice. The scientific theories accepted by the community of inquirers at a given time do, of course, have ontological commitments. A particular theory is not ontologically neutral. But because what is accepted at one time is modified or rejected at a later time, the ontology of science is a work in progress. The concept of science is not the concept of any particular ontology.

In early modern philosophy, the ontology of science included reference to God and his supernatural activities; just look at the way in which scientific reasoning was strongly connected to theological doctrines in the work of Descartes, Leibniz, and Newton; the correspondence between

Leibniz and Samuel Clarke illustrates this very well. The reason why the current ontology of science is naturalistic (as opposed to super-naturalistic) is that criticisms (e.g., by Hume and Kant) have raised doubts about the arguments, empirical and a priori, for God's existence, and various scientific theories such as natural selection and the big bang have seemed to show that theological backing is unnecessary and unsupported by empirical evidence. What determines the ontology of science at any given time is experience, experiment, and logical thinking, not a prescription emanating from the very idea of science.

ACTIVE AGENCY

Thus far I have argued that the evidence supports the reality of free will when this means that people are capable of deciding among alternatives on the basis of deliberation, that such decisions are effective, and that the reality of choice entails that persons are capable of doing otherwise and for that reason are responsible for their actions. Understood in this way, free will implies that, contrary to Laplace's dictum, the anterior state of the universe is not invariably a sufficient causal condition for subsequent states.

However, that conclusion does not entail that causality does not enter into choice and action at all. I recommend returning to the Aristotelian tradition and thinking of the person as an active substance or agent capable of initiating sequences of changes not determined by sufficient conditions of the past. This is what Locke called *active power*, wherein an agent is the efficient cause of the changes following from its acts of will.[23] Deliberation, decision, and choice are not caused by antecedent sufficient conditions but are acts of the agent who deliberates, decides, and chooses. Concerning any free action, we can ask: Who did it? How was it done? Why was it done? What are its consequences? Answers to these questions provide an exposition of a free action. They provide all that is necessary to explain, understand, and interpret the action itself.[24] Historians and biographers as well as others are interested in expositions of the actions of the persons they study. To discover the reasons that lie behind the observable behavior and discourse of their subjects involves entering into their mental life by reconstructing the deliberative processes that influenced their decisions and plans. In order to do this, Hobbes recommends "*Read thy self*": "whosoever looketh into himself, and considereth what he doth, when he does *think, opine, reason, hope, feare,* etc., and upon what grounds; he shall thereby read and know, what are the thoughts, and Passions of all other men, upon the like occasions."[25] The first-person point of view provides the basic understanding of active agency and human motivation that constitutes the framework for interpreting the actions of others. But should it turn out that there were antecedent sufficient causal conditions of the choice and decision, then what was done was not really an action, the person who did it was not an active agent, and there was merely the illusion, not the reality, of choice and decision.

A view popular among philosophers sympathetic to physicalism is that the physical universe is closed. "One way of stating the principle of physical causal closure is this: If you pick any physical event and trace out its causal ancestry or posterity, that will never take you outside the physical domain."[26] This hypothesis of closure implies that if mind cannot be reduced to matter, then a person cannot act thoughtfully: his thoughts and deliberations are ineffective epiphenomena. There is even the appearance of a scientific argument in favor of closure in the doctrine of the conservation of energy. If energy is conserved, then there cannot be any nonphysical interventions in nature because these would increase the total quantity of energy, contrary to the principle of conservation.

However, the principle of the conservation of energy applies to the physical world taken in abstraction from any possible nonphysical interventions. The principle of closure is at best an abstraction: energy is conserved within physical nature. It does not exclude the possibility that if there are interventions originating in nonphysical activities, the total energy in nature is increased. After all, the conservation principle is supported by theoretical considerations and local experiments, not by the actual measurement of the total amount of energy in the physical universe at different times. Therefore, the principle cannot be employed to support either physicalism or epiphenomenalism. There is, I conclude, no scientific reason to deny the reality of active agency; there is no scientific reason that outweighs our experience of deliberation, choice, and decision in establishing the reality of the intermingling of mind and body. There is no reason for supposing that active power is an illusion. Experience supports the claim that mental causation is a fact and not an illusion and that mental acts are not merely supervenient upon physical processes but are capable of initiating sequences of physical events in their own right.

Moreover, it is mere prejudice to think that a materialist conception of the self is capable of providing a more intelligible representation of agency than a dualistic conception. After all, for physicalism, the self is just a physical organism, and this is reducible to a bunch of interacting molecules. How choice and decision fit into this picture is more of a puzzle than how they fit into the interactionist model of Descartes. Locke pointed out that "*Person* . . . is a Forensick Term appropriating Actions and their Merit; and so belongs only to intelligent Agents capable of a Law, and Happiness and Misery."[27] I see no way that a framework of thought that conceives living human animals as simply a bunch of molecules interacting according to physical law can account for persons in this sense. No doubt, persons and minds emerge in part from the natural order in ways that are not well understood, but that does not mean that they are reducible to the physicalistic scheme of things. One further major advantage of the Cartesian picture is that it enables its advocates to resist the temptation to deny the reality of facts whose existence introspection and experience confirm every moment of our waking lives. By surrendering the effort to reduce mind to matter, one is in a position to offer full and unqualified recognition to the existence of thinking things, to their freedom, and to their moral autonomy.

FINAL THOUGHTS

Throughout these five chapters, I have taken a stand in favor of a dualistic account of the self and the relation between mind and body. Obviously I am convinced that dualism is true and that rival theories such as materialism, reductive physicalism, and idealism are false. However, the views I reject have many staunch defenders who think that dualism is neither true nor plausible. They believe that they have science, currently the most prestigious basis of belief, on their side, whereas I have rejected a view of science that associates it with materialism.

This is not a new debate. It started when Western philosophical thought was in its infancy. There were materialists among the ancient philosophers—Democritus, Epicurus, and Lucretius are prominent examples—and there were others—Plato and Aristotle—who rejected materialism and opted for one or another version of dualism. Fierce debates about the nature of mind and its relation to bodily functions have marked every period of Western thought, and one finds similar disagreements within Eastern philosophy.

So it is unlikely that these chapters or any other subsequent contributions will bring to an end what really is a persistent, interminable, and fundamental disagreement not only among philosophers but generally among those who have put their minds to the problem. Since the debate spills over into other topics and disagreements in ethics and religion, in epistemology and metaphysics, there is plenty of fuel to keep aglow the flames of debate and argumentation.

But what explains the persistence of the disagreement on these issues as well as on philosophical topics in general? Most questions that we ask about matters of fact can be resolved in less than two millennia. Why do philosophical disputes persist without closure, considering that many of the great philosophers of the past have thought that their systems have finally settled all outstanding issues? Descartes claimed that he had settled once and for all of the fundamental questions of metaphysics. Wittgenstein, in his 1922 publication *Tractatus Logico-Philosophicus,* asserts in the preface that "the *truth* of the thoughts that are here communicated seems to me unassailable and definitive. I therefore believe myself to have found, on all essential points, the final solution of the problems."[28] But in the preface to his *Philosophical Investigations,* published posthumously in 1953, he writes, "I have been forced to recognize grave mistakes in what I wrote in that first book."[29]

Philosophers no longer claim finality for their theories or arguments. The quest for certainty identified with Plato and Descartes has given way to a fallibilistic outlook that accepts the absence of finality as a normal feature of philosophical discourse. But this lack of finality and conclusiveness of philosophical argument is not sufficient to explain the long-term persistence of disagreement; the hard sciences are frequently able to arrive at a general consensus about fundamentals, even though it is understood that new data and theories may overturn prevailing points of view.

I find two major sources of the persistence of philosophical disagreement. In the first place, there are reasons for disagreement external to philosophical inquiry that are themselves interminable, such as religious disagreement and ideological conflict. The ideals and prejudices of people, expressing how they want the world to be, are capable of embedding themselves into issue-oriented discussions and swerving thought away from the independent momentum of reason, if there is such a thing. In particular, the arguments between materialism, dualism, idealism, and other ontologies have, over time, been swayed by the strong associations between conceptions of the person and religious beliefs. It is possible to isolate the discussion from such ideals and ideologies, as I have attempted to do in this book, but one can never be sure that one has succeeded, and perhaps it is not possible for thought to take place if one abstracts from all presuppositions and preferred perspectives. Perhaps there is no such thing as the independent momentum of reason; perhaps reason itself can never catch up with its presuppositions in order to capture them in its embrace. Perhaps the commitment to prior doctrine and method is unavoidable even in sincere and self-conscious attempts to be rational.

In the second place, there are reasons for persistence that are internal to the process of philosophical inquiry itself. Consider the arguments over free will that have been touched upon in this chapter. I have argued in behalf of the libertarian position that rejects determinism and asserts that choice and decision have no antecedent sufficient condition other than the activities of the agent. Compatibilism and soft determinism agree with libertarianism that there is such a thing as free will, but the former claims that free will and determinism can coexist, whereas the latter goes further and asserts that determinism is true. This disagreement does not revolve around a few isolated matters of fact but pertains to the very nature of choice, decision, and active agency. A purely factual disagreement as to whether, for example, this person decided to perform that action may easily be resolvable by prevailing commonsense methods of fixing belief. But disagreements about the nature of human decision making itself and its presuppositions are interminable because the very methods of fixing belief are among the topics at issue.

Suppose after centuries of intense discussion among advocates of these three positions, they are able to agree about the nature of free will and active agency. Even then a fourth point of view, hard determinism, is ready to obstruct this pleasant outcome and deny what these three agree upon, namely, the existence of free will itself. That is, the very phenomenon whose explanation brought these disagreements into play is rejected. It is as if in physics, after a consensus has been formed upon the molecular structure of some substance, an irritable physicist calls into question the very existence of the substance or even the existence of molecules. In physics, however, such a wayward voice would receive no hearing, whereas in philosophy, wayward voices are frequently welcomed as deepening the discussion, opening up new ways of going forward, and revealing fruitful perspectives that cannot be ignored.

The persistence of philosophical disagreement suggests to me a way of looking at philosophical argumentation that differs from its surface appearance. At first glance, philosophers seem to be offering arguments to prove the truth of the positions they have adopted, even to arrive at the sort of certainty that Descartes claimed for the *Cogito.* Instead, their arguments should be looked upon as essentially apologetic or defensive in nature. They have the effect not of providing final proofs of a doctrinal conclusion but of preserving the cogency of the doctrine at issue by warding off the blows of those who reject it and thus maintaining its plausibility, preserving its base, and perhaps gaining some converts. We see this in theological, political, and ethical disputes as well as in philosophy. I am not here adopting a skeptical stance, as if philosophical finality were impossible. In fact, at various times it was widely believed that finality had been achieved. Many philosophers came to believe, for example, that Russell's theory of descriptions resolved once and for all the puzzle over apparent reference to nonexistent entities and that Moore's open question argument finally disposed of naturalism in ethics. But they were soon to be disappointed: alternative versions and rationales of the doomed theories brought them back to life, and new approaches made it clear that the theories of Russell and Moore were prominent contenders rather than winners by a knockout. The life of philosophy consists not of frequent funerals for dead theories, but of happy celebrations of recoveries from illness.

Notes

INTRODUCTION

My use of "he/his" throughout this work is intended to be gender neutral except in those cases in which it actually designates a male.

1. Arthur O. Lovejoy, *The Revolt Against Dualism: An Inquiry Concerning the Existence of Ideas* (La Salle, Ill.: Open Court, 1955), 33.

Chapter One. BODY AND MIND

1. René Descartes, *The Philosophical Writings of Descartes,* trans. John Cottingham, Robert Stoothoff, and Dugald Murdoch, 3 vols. (Cambridge: Cambridge University Press, 1984), 2:349.

2. For a discussion of the problem of the criterion in ancient Greek philosophy, see Sextus Empiricus, *Outlines of Pyrrhonism,* trans. R. G. Bury (Buffalo, N.Y.: Prometheus Books, 1990). For a general discussion of the problem, see Charles Landesman, *Skepticism: The Central Issues* (Oxford: Blackwell Publishers, 2002), chapters 5 and 6.

3. Descartes, *Philosophical Writings,* 2:17.

4. Here is another way of looking at the *Cogito.* "He [Samuel Beckett] loved the tension in *cogito ergo sum* and took a dim view of the connecting word, the *ergo* in the equation. Cogitating was the nightmare from which his characters were trying to awake. Being was a sour trick played on them by some force with which they are trying desperately not to reckon. Beckett produced infinite amounts of comedy about the business of thinking as boring, invalid, and quite unnecessary.

His characters did not need to think in order to be, or be in order to think. They knew they existed because of the odd habits and deep discomforts of their bodies. I itch therefore I am." Colm Tóibín, "Happy Birthday, Sam!" *The New York Review of Books,* April 27, 2006, 24–25.

5. Descartes, *Philosophical Writings,* 2:19.

6. Ibid.

7. Ibid.

8. Ibid.

9. Ibid., 2:56.

10. Ibid., 2:57.

11. The first use of the term 'qualia' (singular 'quale') that I am familiar with to designate sensory items occurs throughout C. I. Lewis's *Mind and the World Order* (New York: Dover Publications, 1956) [first published in 1929]. He understands them to be universals that are repeatable from one experience to another. Under the influence of the writings of Bertrand Russell and G. E. Moore, the term 'sense-datum' became widely used. As a result of criticisms of the sense-datum theory, those who accept sense-data but dare not speak its name tend now to use 'quale'.

12. Descartes, *Philosophical Writings,* 2:6–7.

13. Ibid., 2:59.

14. Ibid., 2:234.

15. Ibid., 2:51.

16. Ibid., 2:265.

17. Jaegwon Kim, *Mind in a Physical World* (Cambridge: MIT Press, 2000), 57.

18. Descartes, *Philosophical Writings,* 2:235.

19. Ibid., 2:236.

20. Ibid., 2:237. Gassendi's quote is from Lucretius, *De Rerum Natura* I.305.

21. Descartes, *Philosophical Writings,* 2:238.

22. Ibid., 2:239.

23. Ibid., 2:275.

24. Quoted in Howard Stein, "Newton's Metaphysics," in *The Cambridge Companion to Newton,* ed. I. Bernard Cohen and George F. Smith (Cambridge: Cambridge University Press, 2002), 267–68.

25. Colin McGinn, "Can We Ever Understand Consciousness?" *New York Review of Books,* June 10, 1999, 45, 47.

26. G. W. Leibniz, *Philosophical Essays,* trans. Roger Ariew and Daniel Garber (Indianapolis: Hackett Publishing Co., 1989), 215.

27. Quine has discussed this in many places; for a brief presentation of his overall point of view on this question, see his "Speaking of Objects," in *Ontological Relativity and Other Essays* (New York: Columbia University Press, 1969).

28. John Searle, *Intentionality* (Cambridge: Cambridge University Press, 1983), 268.

29. John Locke, *Essay concerning Human Understanding,* ed. Peter H. Nidditch (Oxford: Clarendon Press, 1975), IV.x.16.

30. This suggestion was offered by an anonymous reviewer.

31. For a detailed critique of physicalistic functionalism along these lines, see Ned Block, "Troubles with Functionalism," in *Minnesota Studies in the Philosophy of Science,* vol. 9, ed. C. Wade Savage (Minneapolis: University of Minnesota Press, 1978).

32. Unlike Descartes, Leibniz rejected mind/body intermingling and interaction in favor of a preestablished harmony underwritten by God.

33. Leibniz, *Philosophical Essays,* 223.

34. Ibid., 83.

35. Locke, *Essay,* III.iii.1.

Chapter Two. OTHER MINDS

1. Descartes, *Philosophical Writings,* 1:140.

2. Ibid.

3. Ibid.

4. A. M. Turing, "Computing Machinery and Intelligence," *Mind* 59, no. 236 (October 1950): 433–60.

5. Searle, *Intentionality,* 27.

6. Walter Bagehot, *Shakespeare the Man* (New York: McCure Phillips and Co., 1901), 36.

7. Ludwig Wittgenstein, *Philosophical Investigations,* 3rd ed., trans. G. E. M. Anscombe (New York: Macmillan, 1958), Part I, #293. Hereafter *PI.*

8. For a discussion of certain qualifications on this first condition, see Charles Landesman, *The Eye and the Mind: Reflections on Perception and the Problem of Knowledge* (Dordrecht: Kluwer Academic Publishers, 1993), 130–32.

9. Wittgenstein, *PI,* Part I, #485.

10. Charles Sanders Peirce, *Collected Papers of Charles Sanders Peirce,* ed. Charles Hartshorne and Paul Weiss (Cambridge, Mass.: Harvard University Press, 1931–1935), vol. 1, par. 171.

11. W. V. Quine, "Two Dogmas of Empiricism," in *From a Logical Point of View* (New York: Harper and Row, 1961), 42–43.

12. Ibid., 43.

13. Ibid., 44.

14. Alfred North Whitehead, *Process and Reality,* corrected edition, ed. David Ray Griffin and Donald W. Sherburne (New York: Free Press, 1978), 91.

15. Wittgenstein, *PI,* Part I, #293.
16. Ibid., #303.
17. Ibid., #304.
18. Ibid.
19. Ibid., #305.
20. Ibid., #304.
21. Ibid.
22. Ibid., #293.
23. Ibid., #308.
24. Ibid., #1.
25. Quine, "Two Dogmas," 18.
26. Quine, *Ontological Relativity,* 72.
27. For further discussion of skepticism, see Landesman, *Skepticism.*
28. Thomas Reid, *Essays on the Intellectual Powers of Man,* in *Philosophical Works,* ed. Sir William Hamilton (Hildesheim: Georg Olms Verlagbuchhandlung, 1967), vol. 1, 449.
29. Ibid., 450.
30. Ibid., 449–50.
31. Ibid., 449.
32. Ibid., 449, 450.
33. Ibid., 450.
34. Ibid.
35. For a defense of the language of thought, see Jerry Fodor, *The Language of Thought* (New York: Thomas Y. Crowell, 1975).
36. Donald Davidson, *Subjective, Intersubjective, Objective* (Oxford: Clarendon Press, 2001), 124, 130.
37. Wittgenstein, *PI,* Part I, #329.
38. Ibid., #332.
39. Ibid., #335.
40. Lewis Carroll, *Through the Looking Glass,* chapter 6, in *The Annotated Alice,* introduction and notes by Martin Gardner (Cleveland and New York: World Publishing, 1969), 269.
41. Wittgenstein, *PI,* Part I, #665.

Chapter Three. SELF-CONSCIOUSNESS AND THOUGHT

1. Descartes, *Philosophical Writings,* 2:100.
2. Ibid., 2:171–72.
3. Locke, *Essay,* II.i.4.
4. Peirce, *Collected Papers,* 2: par. 382n.

5. One reader has pointed out that it would be incompatible with PTT to interpret such traces as current, though unconscious, acts of thought. He is correct on this point, and this suggests that Descartes' conception of mind would need to be modified and/or supplemented in order to be made compatible with Freud's dynamic unconscious.

6. Descartes, *Philosophical Writings,* 2:156.

7. Ibid., 2:124.

8. Friedrich Nietzsche, *Beyond Good and Evil,* in *Basic Writings of Nietzsche,* trans. Walter Kaufmann (New York: Modern Library, 1968), 213.

9. David Hume, *A Treatise of Human Nature,* ed. L. A. Selby-Bigge (Oxford: Clarendon Press, 1951), I.i.6.

10. Ibid., I.iv.6.

11. Henry Clarke Warren, *Buddhism In Translation* (New York: Atheneum, 1963), 133–34.

12. Ibid., 146.

13. Ibid., 152.

14. William James, *The Principles of Psychology* (New York: Dover Publications, 1950), 2:296.

15. Ibid., 2:238.

16. Ibid., 2:242.

17. Ibid., 2:400–401.

18. Wittgenstein mentions Lichtenberg's remark in a lecture recorded by G. E. Moore, *Philosophical Papers* (New York: Collier Books, 1962), 100–101.

19. Whitehead, *Process and Reality,* 7.

20. Nietzsche, *Beyond Good and Evil,* 214.

21. Steven Pinker, *The Blank Slate: The Modern Denial of Human Nature* (New York: Viking, 2002), 42–43.

22. Ibid., 43.

23. Ibid.

24. For a discussion of the automaton theory, see William James, *Principles,* chapter 5.

25. Martin Heidegger, *Being and Time,* trans. John Macquarrie and Edward Robinson (London: SCM Press, 1962), 34.

26. Ibid., 46.

27. Ibid.

28. Ibid., 73.

29. Ibid., 74.

30. For Locke's discussion of personal identity, see *Essay,* II.xxvii.

31. Butler's view is contained in his dissertation "Of Personal Identity," and Reid's in passages in his *Essays on the Intellectual Powers of Man.* Both are included in John Perry, ed., *Personal Identity* (Berkeley: University of California Press, 1975).

Chapter Four. PERCEPTUAL CONSCIOUSNESS

1. G. E. Moore, "The Refutation of Idealism," in *Philosophical Studies* (London: Routledge and Kegan Paul, 1922), 20.
2. Ibid.
3. Ibid., 25.
4. Ibid.
5. This is the view of B. A. Farrell, "Experience," in *The Philosophy of Mind,* ed. V. C. Chappell (Englewood Cliffs, N.J.: Prentice-Hall, 1962).
6. Moore, "Refutation of Idealism," 29.
7. Ibid., 27.
8. Moore, *Philosophical Studies,* viii.
9. See Thomas Nagel, "What Is It Like to Be a Bat?" *Philosophical Review* (October 1974): 435–50.
10. William Broad, "It's Sensitive Really," *New York Times,* Science Section, December 13, 2005.
11. G. E. Moore, "A Defense of Common Sense," in *Philosophical Papers* (New York: Collier Books, 1962), 44.
12. P. F. Strawson, *Individuals: An Essay in Descriptive Metaphysics* (London: Methuen, 1959), 9.
13. Ibid., 10.
14. Ibid.
15. Wilfrid Sellars, *Science, Perception and Reality* (London: Routledge and Kegan Paul, 1963), 27.
16. David Hume, *Enquiry concerning Human Understanding,* Section XII, Part i, in *Enquiries concerning the Human Understanding and concerning the Principles of Morals,* ed. L. A. Selby-Bigge (Oxford: Clarendon Press, 1902).
17. For the claim that all seeing is seeing that, see Searle, *Intentionality,* 40, and John McDowell, *Mind and World* (Cambridge, Mass.: Harvard University Press, 1994), 29.
18. Lewis, *Mind and the World Order,* 66.
19. See Charles S. Peirce, *The Essential Pierce: Selected Philosophical Writings* (Bloomington: Indiana University Press, 1998), 2:442, 461, 481.
20. Whitehead, *Process and Reality,* 61.
21. Locke, *Essay,* IV.xxi.4.
22. Ibid., II.viii.12.
23. Ibid., II.viii.10.
24. Ibid., IV.iii.16.
25. Ibid., II.viii.9, 10.
26. Max Weber, *From Max Weber,* ed. H. H. Gerth and C. Wright Mills (New York: Oxford University Press, 1958), 350.

27. Alfred North Whitehead, *Science and the Modern World* (New York: Free Press, 1967), 54.

28. Locke, *Essay,* II.viii.16.

29. Ibid., II.viii.15.

30. For Sellars' distinction between these two images, see his "Philosophy and the Scientific Image of Man," in *Science, Perception and Reality,* 1–40.

31. Locke, *Essay,* II.viii.16.

32. Thomas Hobbes, *The Elements of Law, Natural and Politic,* ed. Ferdinand Tönnies (Cambridge: Cambridge University Press, 1928), 274.

33. Thomas Hobbes, *Leviathan* (Oxford: Clarendon Press, 1952), Book 1, chapter 1.

34. Whitehead, *Science,* 52.

35. Ibid., 148.

36. Ibid., 51.

37. Sellars, "Empiricism and the Philosophy of Mind," in *Science, Perception and Reality,* 172–73.

38. Ibid., 173.

39. Whitehead, *Science,* 87.

40. Ibid., 83.

41. Ibid., 89.

42. Ibid., 219.

43. Hermann Weyl, *The Open World* (New Haven: Yale University Press, 1934), 6–7.

44. "A new theory . . . is seldom or never just an increment to what is already known. Its assimilation requires the reconstruction of prior theory and the re-evaluation of prior fact." Thomas S. Kuhn, *The Structure of Scientific Revolutions,* 2d ed. (Chicago: University of Chicago Press, 1970), 7.

45. Lewis, *Mind and the World Order,* 66.

46. Hume, *Treatise,* I.iv.2.

47. Quine, *Ontological Relativity,* 82.

48. McDowell, *Mind and World,* 134.

49. I do not want to deny that there are cases where thought influences the sensory order. Some experiments suggest that not only are there bottom-up influences of the sensory order upon thought, but also there are top-down influences of thought upon the sensory order. See, for example, "3,2,1: This Is Your Brain under Hypnosis," *New York Times,* Science Section, November 22, 2005. Expectations may sometimes influence the character of the qualia and their organization. But the top-down causal influences of thought upon sense data do not entail that the sensory order is inherently conceptualized.

50. Durant Drake et al., *Essays in Critical Realism* (New York: Macmillan, 1920), 172.

51. Ibid., 168n.
52. Ibid., 21.
53. Ibid., 241.
54. Ibid.
55. Ibid., 243–44.

Chapter Five. AGENCY

1. Hobbes, *Leviathan,* Part I, chapter 6.

2. Thomas Reid points out that the attempt on the part of philosophers to reduce will to desire "tends to confound things which are very different in their nature." For a full discussion of the difference between will and desire, see chapter 1 of Essay 2 of Reid's *Essays on the Active Powers of Man* (1788), in *Philosophical Works,* vol. 2, ed. Sir William Hamilton (Hildesheim: Georg Olms Verlagbuchhandlung, 1967).

3. Note how thin is William James' conception of the will in comparison with this functional approach: "Attention with effort is all that any case of volition implies. *The essential achievement of the will, in short, when it is most 'voluntary,' is to attend to a difficult object and hold it fast before the mind.* The doing so *is* the *fiat*" (*Principles of Psychology,* 2:561). James is, however, quite correct in insisting that paying attention to something is essentially an act of will.

4. Conscience cannot be identified with Freud's superego, incidentally, because conscience may come to oppose the values of family and society internalized in the superego.

5. William James advises us to distinguish between "the possibles which really tempt a man and those which tempt him not at all" (*Principles of Psychology,* 2:577n).

6. Donald Davidson, "Actions, Reasons, and Causes," in *The Philosophy of Action,* ed. Alan R. White (London: Oxford University Press, 1968), 85.

7. Ibid.

8. Ibid., 86.

9. Ibid., 87.

10. In his *On Selfhood and Godhood* (New York: Macmillan, 1957), Lectures 8–10, C. A. Campbell defends a view of free will that has influenced my account considerably. However, he restricts the exercise of freedom to the situation in which there is a conflict between desire and moral duty, whereas I see no reason for such a restriction. Prudential contexts in which rational self-love (Butler's term) operates often present circumstances of decision as difficult as moral contexts. I see no reason to restrict the exercise of freedom to the occasions of moral choice.

11. Whitehead observes that when the light makes a man's eyes blink, "he feels that the experiences of the *eye* in the matter of the flash are causal of the

blink." In opposition to Hume, Whitehead asserts that "the notion of causation arose because mankind lives amid experiences in the mode of causal efficacy." Hume was simply mistaken in thinking that experiences of causal compulsion are reducible to constant conjunction (*Process and Reality,* 175). There is, in certain cases, a direct experience of causality that provides a conception of causality that can be extended to instances in which conscious experience is absent.

12. Thus Schopenhauer asserts, "All motives are causes, . . . and all causality carries with it necessity" (*Essay on the Freedom of the Will,* trans. Konstantin Kolenda [Indianapolis: Bobbs-Merrill, 1960], 36). He adds, "Every action of a man is the necessary product of his character and of the operating motive. Given both of them, the effect follows inevitably" (58).

13. The weight or strength of a reason should be thought of not by analogy with a physical or mental force but logically, as how persuasive the reason is to the agent. Its weight is not something merely discovered; it is often determined in the act of choice. Thus, Schopenhauer is on to something when he says: "In any difficult choice, our own resolve, like that of another person, remains a mystery to us until the choice has actually been made" (*Essay on the Freedom of the Will,* 50).

14. Should we go along with Victor Frankl when he says that "a person is free to shape his own character, and man is responsible for what he may have made out of himself"? (*Will to Meaning* [New York: Meridian, 1988], 17). And with C. A, Campbell, who claims, "The agent believes that through his act of decision he can oppose and transcend his own formed character in the interests of duty"? (*In Defence of Free Will* [London: George Allen and Unwin, 1967], 43).

15. Descartes, *Philosophical Writings,* 2:19.

16. Quoted in Patrick Suppes, *Probabilistic Metaphysics* (Oxford: Basil Blackwell, 1984), 17.

17. Donald Davidson, *Essays on Actions and Events* (Oxford: Clarendon Press, 1980), 208.

18. Schopenhauer asks "whether man alone constitutes an exception to the whole of nature" (*Essay on the Freedom of the Will,* 17). He answers: "The actions of men, like everything else in nature, take place in any given case as an effect which follows necessarily" (25). But if indeterminism is true, then not everything takes place as an effect which follows necessarily. In that respect, the human person does not constitute an exception to the whole of nature.

19. Suppes, *Probabilistic Metaphysics,* 11.

20. Ibid., 27.

21. Ibid., 29.

22. "Man's freedom is no freedom from conditions but rather freedom to take a stand on whatever conditions might confront him" (Frankl, *Will to Meaning,* 16).

23. Locke, *Essay,* II.xxi.4–5. See also Campbell, *In Defence of Free Will,* 50–51.

24. Schopenhauer claims that indeterminism implies that "every human action would be an inexplicable miracle—an effect without a cause" (*Essay on the Freedom of the Will,* 47). However, no miracle is implied because an exposition of an action makes it intelligible in the way appropriate for products of human choice.

25. Hobbes, Introduction to *Leviathan.*

26. Kim, *Mind in a Physical World,* 40.

27. Locke, *Essay,* II.xxvii.26.

28. Ludwig Wittgenstein, *Tractatus Logico-Philosophicus,* trans. D. F. Pears and B. F. McGuinness (New York: Humanities Press, 1972), 5.

29. Wittgenstein, *PI,* vi.

Bibliography

Bagehot, Walter. *Shakespeare the Man.* New York: McClure Phillips and Co., 1901.

Block, Ned. "Troubles with Functionalism." In *Minnesota Studies in the Philosophy of Science.* Vol. 9. Edited by C. Wade Savage. Minneapolis: University of Minnesota Press, 1978.

Campbell, C. A. *In Defence of Free Will.* London: George Allen and Unwin, 1967.

———. *On Selfhood and Godhood.* New York: Macmillan, 1957.

Carroll, Lewis. *Through the Looking Glass.* In *The Annotated Alice.* Introduction and Notes by Martin Gardner. Cleveland and New York: World Publishing, 1969.

Davidson, Donald. "Actions, Reasons, and Causes." In *The Philosophy of Action.* Edited by Alan R. White. London: Oxford University Press, 1968.

———. *Essays on Actions and Events.* Oxford: Clarendon Press, 1980.

———. *Subjective, Intersubjective, Objective.* Oxford: Clarendon Press, 2001.

Descartes. René. *The Philosophical Writings of Descartes.* Translated by John Cottingham, Robert Stoothoff, and Dugald Murdoch. 3 vols. Cambridge: Cambridge University Press, 1984.

Drake, Durant, et al. *Essays in Critical Realism.* New York: Macmillan, 1920.

Farrell, B. A. "Experience." In *The Philosophy of Mind.* Edited by V. C. Chappell. Englewood Cliffs, N.J.: Prentice-Hall, 1962.

Fodor, Jerry. *The Language of Thought.* New York: Thomas Y. Crowell, 1975.

Frankl, Victor. *Will to Meaning.* New York: Meridian, 1988.

Heidegger, Martin. *Being and Time.* Translated by John Macquarrie and Edward Robinson. London: SCM Press, 1962.

Hobbes, Thomas. *The Elements of Law, Natural and Politic.* Edited by Ferdinand Tönnies. Cambridge: Cambridge University Press, 1928.

———. *Leviathan.* Oxford: Clarendon Press, 1952.

Hume, David. *A Treatise of Human Nature.* Edited by L. A. Selby-Bigge. Oxford: Clarendon Press, 1951.

———. *Enquiry concerning Human Understanding.* In *Enquiries concerning the Human Understanding and concerning the Principles of Morals.* Edited by L. A. Selby-Bigge. Oxford: Clarendon Press, 1902.

James, William. *The Principles of Psychology.* 2 vols. New York: Dover Publications, 1950.

Kant, Immanuel. *Critique of Pure Reason.* Translated by Norman Kemp Smith. New York: St. Martin's Press, 1965.

Kim, Jaegwon. *Mind in a Physical World.* Cambridge: MIT Press, 2000.

Kuhn, Thomas S. *The Structure of Scientific Revolutions.* 2d ed. Chicago: University of Chicago Press, 1970.

Landesman, Charles. *The Eye and the Mind: Reflections on Perception and the Problem of Knowledge.* Dordrecht: Kluwer Academic Publishers, 1993.

———. *Skepticism: The Central Issues.* Oxford: Blackwell Publishers, 2002.

Leibniz, G. W. *Philosophical Essays.* Translated by Roger Ariew and Daniel Garber. Indianapolis: Hackett Publishing Co., 1989.

Lewis, C. I. *Mind and the World Order.* New York: Dover Publications, 1956.

Locke, John. *Essay concerning Human Understanding.* Edited by Peter H. Nidditch. Oxford: Clarendon Press, 1975.

Lovejoy, Arthur O. *The Revolt against Dualism: An Inquiry concerning the Existence of Ideas.* La Salle, Ill.: Open Court, 1955.

McDowell, John. *Mind and World.* Cambridge, Mass.: Harvard University Press, 1994.

McGinn, Colin. "Can We Ever Understand Consciousness?" *New York Review of Books,* June 10, 1999.

Moore, G. E. *Philosophical Papers.* New York: Collier Books, 1962.

———. *Philosophical Studies.* London: Routledge and Kegan Paul, 1922.

Nagel, Thomas. "What Is It Like to Be a Bat?" *Philosophical Review* 83, no. 4 (October 1974): 435–50.

New York Times. Science Section. November 22, 2005; December 13, 2005.

Nietzsche, Frederick. *Beyond Good and Evil.* In *Basic Writings of Nietzsche.* Translated by Walter Kaufman. New York: Modern Library, 1968.

Peirce, Charles Sanders. *Collected Papers of Charles Sanders Peirce.* Edited by Charles Hartshorne and Paul Weiss. 6 vols. Cambridge, Mass.: Harvard University Press, 1931–1935.

———. *Essential Peirce: Selected Philosophical Writings.* 2 vols. Bloomington: Indiana University Press, 1992 (vol. 1), 1998 (vol. 2).

Perry, John, ed. *Personal Identity.* Berkeley: University of California Press, 1975.

Pinker, Steven. *The Blank Slate: The Modern Denial of Human Nature.* New York: Viking, 2002.

Quine, W. V. *Ontological Relativity and Other Essays.* New York: Columbia University Press, 1969.

———. "Two Dogmas of Empiricism." In *From a Logical Point of View.* New York: Harper and Row, 1961.

Reid, Thomas, *Essays on the Active Powers of Man.* In *Thomas Reid, Philosophical Works.* Vol. 2. Edited by Sir William Hamilton. Hildesheim: Georg Olms Verlagbuchhandlung, 1967.

———. *Essays on the Intellectual Powers of Man.* In *Thomas Reid, Philosophical Works.* Vol. 1. Edited by Sir William Hamilton. Hildesheim: Georg Olms Verlagbuchhandlung, 1967.

Schopenhauer, Arthur. *Essay on the Freedom of the Will.* Translated by Konstantin Kolenda. Indianapolis: Bobbs-Merrill, 1960.

Searle, John. *Intentionality.* Cambridge: Cambridge University Press, 1983.

Sellars, Wilfrid. *Science, Perception and Reality.* London: Routledge and Kegan Paul, 1963.

Sextus Empiricus. *Outlines of Pyrrhonism.* Translated by R. G. Bury. Buffalo, N.Y.: Prometheus Books, 1990 [Cambridge, Mass.: Harvard University Press, 1933].

Stein, Howard. "Newton's Metaphysics." In *The Cambridge Companion to Newton.* Edited by I. Bernard Cohen and George F. Smith. Cambridge: Cambridge University Press, 2002.

Strawson, P. F. *Individuals: An Essay in Descriptive Metaphysics.* London: Methuen, 1959.

Suppes, Patrick. *Probabilistic Metaphysics.* Oxford: Basil Blackwell, 1984.

Turing, A. M. "Computing Machinery and Intelligence." *Mind* 59, no. 236 (October 1950): 433–60.

Warren, Henry Clarke. *Buddhism in Translation.* New York: Atheneum, 1963.

Weber, Max. *From Max Weber.* Edited by H. H. Gerth and C. Wright Mills. New York: Oxford University Press, 1958.

Weyl, Hermann. *The Open World.* New Haven: Yale University Press, 1934.

Whitehead, Alfred North. *Process and Reality.* Corrected edition. Edited by David Ray Griffin and Donald W. Sherburne. New York: Free Press, 1978.

———. *Science and the Modern World.* New York: Free Press, 1967.

Wittgenstein, Ludwig. *Philosophical Investigations.* Translated by G. E. M. Anscombe. 3rd ed. New York: Macmillan, 1958.

———. *Tractatus Logico-Philosophicus.* Translated by D. F. Pears and B. F. McGuinness. New York: Humanities Press, 1972.

Index

CHARLES LANDESMAN

is professor emeritus of philosophy at Hunter College and the philosophy program at the Graduate School of the City University of New York. He is the author and editor of eleven books.